I0059248

Consider this...

"If a quotation in large font with someone's name printed below is printed in a book, does that imply they are more knowledgeable or esteemed than you?"

– TIM MARSH

Obviously, the answer is NO...!
(especially when it is my name below the quotation)

I'm telling you this as I enjoy reading thought and wisdom quotations. You'll find them throughout this book. Please take them for what they are.

As you read this book, remember that it is up to you to define success and the priorities in your life. Never stop learning, always do your best, and enjoy life.

"Genius is one percent inspiration, ninety-nine percent perspiration."

– THOMAS EDISON

Learning from…

Tuition Paid by Others

A Collection of Practical, Real-World Leadership Lessons

TIM MARSH

A Mind the Gap Series Book

Tuition Paid by Others

Copyright © 2021 by TIM MARSH. All rights reserved.

A Mind the Gap Series Book

Without written permission of the respective copyright owner, no part of this publication may be reproduced, distributed, or transmitted in any form or by any means, including photocopying, recording, or other electronic or mechanical methods, without the prior written permission, except in the case of brief quotations embodied in critical reviews and certain other non-commercial uses permitted by copyright law.

Mind the Gap cartoons are Copyright © 2021 by Theresa (T-) McCracken (mchumor.com). She reserves all rights. All cartoons are used with permission. Editing by Kate Burnham of Toronto, ON. Cover art and book formatting by Susan Veach (susanveach.com).

Published by: **ResultSYNERGY, LLC**
www.ResultSYNERGY.com

ISBN: Paperback   978-1-7375390-0-1

          eBook   978-1-7375390-1-8

Library of Congress Control Number: 2021913558

I am truly grateful that we've both made it this far...

Seriously!

You see, if you'd asked about me writing a book at the beginning of my career, I would've told you no way, not for me (*most likely while laughing at the thought*).

One of the obvious reasons I never imagined myself writing a book is that I'm not an eloquent writer. When I was in school, I excelled at math and science, but always struggled with English (*and writing*). My grammar has always been suspect and my vocabulary isn't extensive. So, with these limitations known up front, if you can push past them, I know the content is solid.

So, you're probably asking yourself, what changed my mind about writing this book...?

In retrospect (*although I didn't know it at the time*), I suspect the seed of this book was planted decades ago.

PERSONAL BACKSTORY: For my sixth through eighth grade years, I attended Parkview Middle School in Creve Coeur, Illinois. At the beginning of my seventh grade year, a new teacher, Mrs. Fox, was hired. She taught several of my classes that year and the next.

One of her assignments was for us to write in a spiral notebook journal. I *really, really* hated it. In fact, I made it my personal crusade to rid the seventh grade of having to keep a journal.

In the process, I made her life miserable (*I even think I made her cry at one point*). As part of my efforts, I designed an acronym, **JAWS**, that stood for "Journals **A**re a **W**aste of **S**tudents". I had numbers after **JAWS** (*just like the movie sequels*) listing the things I felt were wasted such as time, paper, brain power, or whatever came to mind that day.

Despite her best efforts, she wasn't able to stop my crusade. Even the principal was unable to convince me to stop. (*What he didn't know is all he had to do is call my mom and it would have ceased immediately. She, all five foot four inches, was a force not to be reckoned with when it came to misbehavior, especially in school.*)

As the school year was coming to an end, I asked Mrs. Fox to sign my yearbook (*in pencil*). She wrote "No more journals." and put a little frown face (*which I erased*).

In retrospect, while I really did hate writing in a journal, I regret how I treated her (*especially considering that most of my bad behavior was that of a stupid adolescent boy who had a crush on his teacher and was looking for attention of any kind*).

Years later (*after I graduated from college and had started my career*), I reached out to Mrs. Fox and apologized for my behavior.

I'm going to send her a copy of this book. I hope she laughs at the irony.

The original idea for this book occurred while I was searching for *real-world, practical business knowledge* resources that would help me as a young leader (*keep in mind that I had just graduated, so I thought all knowledge was contained in books*).

What I found then (*and today*) were countless books from well-known authors describing the pathway to becoming a CEO, methods for growing a company, or a combination of both.

While useful, they weren't what I was searching for.

This is the book I sought all those years ago. It provides practical, real-world lessons that were learned from someone who's been there.

The lessons are basic yet fundamental. They are equivalent to the childhood lesson...

Don't put your finger in a light socket.

Early in my career, I suspected that business wasn't significantly different from life in that those who could learn from the successes and failures of others would have an advantage over those who can't.

Over twenty years later, I now know this is absolutely true. I also know that the earlier you can develop this skill, the more potential you have for success.

It's not that the stories about running a multi-billion dollar company are never useful, but what I really wanted (*and needed*) was different. I needed help building my fundamental leadership principles. I wanted something practical that I could immediately put to use.

So voilà, I've now written a book that does both.

Actually, a collection of stories and lessons learned may be a more accurate description. Regardless, I feel confident that this book is a good first step towards providing you the *real-world, practical business knowledge* that I was seeking all those years ago.

The stories and lessons learned in this book are personal and describe actual events. They span my nearly three decades of employment. During that time, I have worked many jobs from a part-time cart attendant to an executive and business owner.

Throughout, I've changed the names of the people involved. In a few cases, I have also redacted (*or modified*) sensitive information. All of these efforts were made to protect the innocent, the guilty, and sometimes quite frankly, the *stupid*…!

In addition to the stories and lessons learned, at the end of each chapter I have included a **Bridging the Gap** subchapter. These subchapters introduce general leadership principles (*although not necessarily associated with the chapter story*). Also interspersed are **Closing the Gap** Leadership Tips. These are meant to inspire positive leadership qualities.

> **DISCLAIMER:** I apologize in advance for any memory lapses or embellishments (*good or bad*) of the true events contained within this book.
>
> I've tried to recall all the facts accurately and to convey them without bias. Over the course of thirty years of work, I'm sure that some details have alluded me.
>
> I'm also aware that some details may be seen now from a different perspective (*by me or others*). As the author, I have the privilege of present the material from my perspective.
>
> In the end, as the stories they are written here convey the intended business and leadership lessons learned.

Tuition Paid by Others

Table of Contents

"What would you do if you weren't afraid?"

– SHERYL SANDBERG

Tuition Paid by Others

Expanded Table of Contents

Expanded Table of Contents (continued)

Expanded Table of Contents (continued)

Expanded Table of Contents (continued)

Expanded Table of Contents (continued)

"If you really look closely, most overnight successes took a long time."

– STEVE JOBS

Chapter 1:

The Interview

> ## "Whether it's your physical surroundings, the actions and words of others, or simply your gut feelings you get when entering a situation, take note of these observations."

– TIM MARSH

Contemplations:

- *Think about the times you've interviewed for a job. Did any of the questions or comments make a lasting impression as good or bad?*

- *Have you ever passed up an educational opportunity that you now regret? How would you feel if your employer offered you a chance to further your education?*

Mind the Gap

"HONEY, I'VE GOT TO GET GOING.
I'M STILL LOOKING FOR THE FOREST..."

The Story...

Location: Southern Illinois University

It was during my senior year of college that I first met Clint. He was the mining engineering department student advisor (*I was about to obtain my bachelor's degree in mechanical engineering*).

As we talked more, I began to consider a dual major of both mechanical and mining engineering for grad school (*it's worth noting in southern Illinois during the late 90s, coal mining was still a thriving industry*).

> **PERSONAL BACKSTORY:** I have known for as long as I can remember that I wanted to go to college. It was in middle school that I decided that I wanted to study engineering.
>
> Both of my parents were very intelligent, but neither went to college. My dad (*a product of state homes and orphanages*) struggled with his grades throughout school. I remember a time when I saw one of his grade school report cards. He had received all F's, yet they continued to pass him to the next grade. Everyone at the school thought he was intellectually disabled, so they had him tested. He surprised everyone with a near genius IQ. Perhaps the topic of another book, his challenge was a common one, priority versus ability.
>
> In 1998, I was the first person in my family to graduate with a college degree. Since then, one of my sisters went back to school recently and obtained a degree.

One day, while we were talking, Clint told me that he was trying to get some '*good*' students to interview with a company that was recruiting on campus for the first time. He asked if I would interview with them. At the time, I was not actively looking for a job, since I planned to attend grad school.

I agreed, not knowing that I would have to pay $25 to register with career services in order to interview. Back then, like many college students, that was a lot of money to spend just to do a favor for a friend. After deciding I really couldn't back out, I paid the fee and completed the registration paperwork. I was set up to attend the evening informational meeting and interview the following day.

Closing the Gap

LEADERSHIP TIP 1:

Lead by example and be a role model for others to follow.

I'm not sure if it was really my decision (*or my mom's insistence*) but I wore the only suit I owned to the informational meeting. I was the first recruit to arrive. Having worn a suit only a few times previously, I was awkward and uncomfortable.

The recruiter's name was Carl. When I arrived, he was already in the large meeting room, setting up for his presentation.

Carl was dressed in khakis and a polo shirt. After introducing myself, he invited me to take off my jacket and have a seat. He told me to make myself comfortable, which I was more than happy to do. I loosened my tie and unbuttoned the top button of my shirt before starting up a conversation.

> **PERSONAL BACKSTORY:** I grew up in a blue collar family with a stay at home mom and a father who punched a factory timeclock every day for over three decades. We were an average middle class working family in those days. When I was growing up, I hardly ever remember wearing a suit. It was only because wearing a suit was required for my senior design presentation that I even owned one.

In those days, I was much more introverted than I am now, so the conversation with Carl was likely as stiff as my shirt.

Eventually, the room began filling up with other students (*many wearing shorts and flip flops*). Unbeknownst to me at the time, the meeting announcement had advertised free pizza and soda, which explained the overwhelming interest.

That interest didn't last long. Within the first few minutes of Carl's presentation, over half of the students got up and left.

> ## Carl was from Abilene. His slide show started out with a desolate west Texas tumbleweed scene. This combined with "it's not uncommon to work 80 hours a week" type comments separated the wheat and chaff pretty quickly despite the free pizza and soda.

I, for better or worse, stayed.

That night after getting home, I immediately shed my suit and began thinking. I knew that companies were looking for people who could observe, assess, and adapt. I decided to wear business casual attire to the interview the next day.

Besides showing that I could observe and adapt, it got me out of wearing a suit. A win-win situation, I thought.

Can you guess what happened?

Yep, I walked into my interview wearing khakis and a polo shirt, only to find Carl wearing a suit. I was flabbergasted. My facial expression must have said everything. Carl started to laugh. He explained that he was only wearing a suit because of a lunch meeting with the Dean after the morning interviews.

PERSONAL BACKSTORY: Years later, I found out that Carl appreciated me for being observant and adapting my attire. He said that it factored into his decision to offer me a second interview.

After three interviews, I was offered a field engineer position. I accepted and Carl and I became friends. We had the opportunity to work together again later in our careers at another company.

...and the Lessons Learned:

- **BE INTENTIONALLY OBSERVANT.**
  Whether it's your physical surroundings, the actions or words of others, or simply your gut feelings when entering a situation, take note of these observations. They are data points that should be considered when making decisions (*in your business and personal life*).

- **INSTINCTIVELY ADAPT TO CHANGE.**
  While there are entire books about change (*and adapting to change*), that's not what I am getting at when I say instinctively adapt to change. What I'm talking about is slightly different and far more personal. It's when adapting to change becomes subconscious (*an instinctive behavior*). It develops from real-life experience of deliberate observation and intentional changes to your actions or words.

Bridging the Gap
Workplace Violence & Bullying

The occurrences and severity of workplace violence and bullying are increasing. While you endeavor to eliminate them, you should mitigate the risk by implementing proactive measures (*such as basic security precautions, appropriate personnel policies, background checks for employees and contractors, and training*).

Incidents of workplace violence and bullying are serious...!

You <u>MUST NOT</u> avoid addressing them as the consequences may be catastrophic.

Bullying is repeated indirect or direct inappropriate behavior. It may be verbal, physical or otherwise, and it can be perpetrated by employees, contractors, vendors, customers, or the general public.

There are four common types of workplace bullying:

- **VERBAL BULLYING.**
  Slander, ridiculing, maligning a person or their family, persistent hurtful name-calling, insulting or humiliating, using someone as the butt of jokes, and abusive or offensive remarks are all types of verbal bullying.

- **PHYSICAL BULLYING.**
  Pushing, shoving, kicking, poking, tripping, physical assault or the threat of physical assault, or damage to a person's work area or property are all types of physical bullying.

- **GESTURE BULLYING.**
  Non-verbal gesture or glance intended to convey a threatening message may be considered gesture bullying.

- **EXCLUSION.**
  Intentionally leaving someone out socially or physically, or disregarding them during work-related activities.

You must ensure that any action that threatens, intimidates, or coerces another employee, customer, vendor, or the general public at work is not tolerated.

IMPORTANT: Bullying occurs in virtually every company and industry. In some industries, bullying has been very prevalent for decades. As a result, it has unfortunately become widely accepted as *'just the way things are'*.

The fact is that you or someone you know may work in an industry where a large percentage of the daily communication could be classified as verbal abuse or where physical contact meant to intimidate another occurs routinely. Just like with other social injustices, bullying is much more common than anyone chooses to acknowledge.

You (*and your company*) must accept that these *'old school'* ways are no longer appropriate in the workplace. No longer should employees be forced to either accept or laugh-off bullying in order to *'fit in with the guys'*.

You must set the expectation and then enforce compliance in order to change. Why? It's no different from the lessons you learned on the grade school playground. There are reasons why people who are bullied often do not report the abuse.

You should be confident that no company resources are allowed to be used to threaten, stalk, or harass anyone. You should treat threats from an abusive personal relationship in a manner similar to any other form of workplace violence.

Protective or Restraining Orders. Personnel policies should include the requirement that employees promptly notify you of any protective or restraining order that they have obtained that lists your company as a protected area. They should also be encouraged to report any safety concerns regarding violent acts by their intimate partner.

Identity and Retaliation. You should promptly investigate all threats of violence or malice, as well as any acts of violence, and bullying. Additionally, you should take necessary precautions to ensure that the identity of anyone reporting bullying, violence threat, or violence incident is protected. In addition, you should take precautions to prevent retaliation against employees making good-faith reports.

In order to maintain workplace safety and the integrity of your investigation, you may find it necessary to suspend employees suspected of bullying, violence, or threats of violence pending the conclusion of the investigation.

Consequences of Workplace Violence and Bullying. Keep in mind that bullying may be intentional or unintentional. Regardless, when an allegation of bullying is made, the intent of the alleged bully shouldn't be a factor during the investigation.

Once your investigation has concluded, anyone found responsible for a bullying or for a violent incident (*including threats*) in violation of your company's HR policies should be subject to prompt and proportionate consequences.

When appropriate, details of the incident and the consequences should be communicated to your employees. The intent of this should be to encourage incident reporting and to discourage inappropriate behaviors.

"A business that makes nothing but money is a poor business."

– Henry Ford

Chapter 2:

Knowledge Suppression

"Leaders that focus on their people and the quality of their products and services usually have a competitive advantage that leads to increased long-term profitability."

– TIM MARSH

Contemplations:

- *Consider the training received when you've started new jobs in the past. Do you feel that it was sufficient? What were the best and worst aspects of the training?*

- *Recall a time in which you lacked the necessary training to do a job effectively. What caused the deficiency? How did the lack of training impact your overall job performance, results, and satisfaction?*

"THE MORE THEY KNOW,
THE MORE WE HAVE TO PAY THEM..."

The Story...
Location: West Virginia

The northeast area operations were a successful family-owned company that had recently been purchased (*our company was a large publicly traded company*). Prior to being acquired, the company had built a basin wide footprint. They commanded a majority of the market share in their primary operating product line due to strong long-term relationships, competitive pricing, and acceptable quality.

I had been discussing the possibility of transitioning out of my Houston based support position back into operations when the opportunity arose to lead the northeast area. From my perspective, the opportunity to move back into operations and closer to family was a no-brainer.

> **PERSONAL BACKSTORY:** The northeast area had seven locations located throughout Illinois, Virginia, Kentucky, West Virginia, and Pennsylvania. The Illinois location was about an hour from family (*both my wife and mine*).
>
> Originally, the plan was for me to manage the northeast area from there, however at the last minute this was denied by corporate. At that point, I was given the option of either staying in my current role or managing the operation from Charleston, West Virginia.
>
> Since Charleston was still eight hours closer to our families, and it would get me back into operations, I chose to move back to West Virginia for the second time in my career.

Prior to the acquisition, the company had operated with a hub and spoke business model. There was a handful of extremely competent owners, managers, and support staff serving as the '*brains*' while the other employees were there to perform the field work (*the labor*). The management, technical knowledge, and support staff (*including all accounting, electronic technicians, fabrication personnel, mechanics, data processing, and safety*), were centrally located. The outlying districts had managers, however they had minimal decision-making authority. They were essentially logistics coordinators.

As part of the transition into my new role, I visited each district as well as some of their field job sites. My primary objective was to meet and get to know the people. I also wanted the opportunity to evaluate the equipment and to get a feel for how well the operations were run.

One of the field job sites I visited had a truck mounted crane in use. Having been in the industry for a long time, I was trained and qualified to operate these type of cranes.

I started casually quizzing the operator and engineer on some basic safety and operational topics. It quickly became obvious that their knowledge was extremely limited.

In fact, both barely understood how to operate the crane. After some additional questions, it was clear that their knowledge was mostly limited to very specific operating procedures (*similar to using a recipe in a cookbook*) and various rules of thumb.

These, such as never lift with the boom angle less than a certain value, allowed employees to complete basic, repetitive jobs with the minimum amount of training. In essence, many field employees knew how to do job tasks, but few understood why.

While the operating procedures and rules of thumb generally kept the operation safe (*as the owner who developed them did have sufficient training*), they did not allow for employees to vary from a limited set of parameters before they were either at a standstill or (*in the worst case*) operating unsafely.

Upon returning to the district office, I continued asking questions and determined that much of the business functioned in a similar way as the crane operations.

This prompted me to ask Shawn, the district operations manager (*and a previous owner*) why the employees were not trained suffi-ciently on the most basic of operations. He replied, "the more they knew, the more we had to pay them".

Closing the Gap

LEADERSHIP TIP 2:

Be humble and know your limits. Be the leader you've always wanted.

Historically, this business model func-tioned, and the operational results were quite good (*hence them being an acquisition target*). The challenge was that now, as a part of our company, this way of operating was no longer acceptable.

The motive to keep the worker's pay low was self-serving on the part of the managers and owners. Prior to the acquisition, the managers consistently qualified for the company's annual bonus program, which required the field operating profit to exceed 50%.

...and the Lessons Learned:

- **PROFITS ARE SIGNIFICANTLY AFFECTED BY SAFETY AND QUALITY.**
  Leaders that focus on their people (*safety*) and the quality of their products and services usually have a competitive advantage that leads to increased long-term profitability.

  On the contrary, leaders that focus on short-term profit-ability by compromising their critical business compo-nents (*safety, quality, marketing, or people*) may meet their objectives but will likely fail long-term.

  Any success achieved with this mode of operation is temporary and irresponsible to your stakeholders.

- **FINANCIAL PERFORMANCE ISN'T THE ONLY FACTOR FOR SUCCESS.**
  In business today, I often see financial performance used as the only factor used to evaluate a company.

  This is a mistake…!

  Successful leaders will take a more detailed look at all aspects of the company in order to determine long-term viability. They understand that the most important factor is people (*which impacts all aspects of business, including financial performance*).

- **INVEST IN YOUR PEOPLE.**
  I know of very few companies with sustained prosperity that reached where they are without having quality people throughout their organization.

  The leaders of these companies know that investing in the knowledge, well-being, and satisfaction of their people is not only decent and humane but also results in the highest probability of long-term success.

Bridging the Gap

Business Gaps

Personnel Gap. The difference between the goals, objectives, and actions of employees that effects results, performance, or job satisfaction.

This gap identifies the misalignment between different groups, including individual employees, employees and management, and teams of employees.

Opportunity Gap. The difference between your current results and the best possible results in your current operating environment.

This gap identifies your potential for improvement (*through mechanisms such as improved processes, procedures, operating efficiency, etc.*) without having to add any additional resources.

Competitive Gap. The difference between your current results and that of a specific competitor.

This gap identifies the potential for improvement based on evaluation of your company (*may include areas such as processes, procedures, personnel competency, training, marketing, products, services, customer base, revenue, profitability, etc.*) with that of a single competitor.

Excellence Gap. The difference between your current results and that of the industry leader.

This gap is similar to the competitor gap and identifies the results of the current industry leading competitor. The purpose is to understand the performance that must be exceeded in order to become the industry leader.

"When companies prioritize their employees' comfort, they are more engaged with increased morale."

– TIM MARSH

"Innovation distinguishes between a leader and follower."

– Steve Jobs

Chapter 3:

The Intent

"While not always possible to overlook a mistake, a person's intent should be considered and grace extended whenever possible when no malicious intent or cause is determined."

– TIM MARSH

Contemplations:

- *Have you ever been pulled over when you were accidentally speeding? Did you feel that you deserved grace because you weren't intentionally violating the law?*

- *Think of a time when you intended one outcome, but a different one occurred instead. Was your intent given any consideration in the aftermath?*

"YOU'RE FIRED UNTIL I CALM DOWN..."

The Story...
Location: Illinois

I started my first official job (*I had mowed lawns and other one-off jobs*) when I was sixteen. They were opening up a new Target store in my hometown, and I was hired as a cashier/cart attendant.

> **PERSONAL BACKSTORY:** I worked at Target all through the remainder of high school and college. During that time, I worked almost every hourly position in the store.
>
> After several years, I was promoted to cashier supervisor, which was my first experience with leading people. I resigned from Target the same week that I graduated from college, moved from Illinois to Texas, and started my professional career.
>
> Interestingly enough, I still remember my Target employee number, **10664829**, over twenty years later.

Except for management and a handful of temporary workers from other stores, we were all new hires. Many of us had never worked in retail before.

After the new hire training, the first few weeks were spent building fixtures and stocking merchandise.

Pallet jacks were one of the types of equipment we used for moving pallets of merchandise. For those of you who don't know, a pallet jack is a device that you can roll into a pallet and pump the handle to lift the pallet. Once lifted, you can then roll the pallet around on the pallet jack wheels.

During one of my first shifts, Ron, the store manager, asked me to take a pallet of merchandise from the stockroom to the front of the store. Eager to complete the task, I grabbed one of the pallet jacks, shoved it in the pallet, pumped the handle to lift it up and tried to pull it towards the front. The issue was the pallet barely moved.

Being a sixteen-year old with more confidence than common sense, I convinced myself that it was so hard to move the pallet because it was so heavy. As a result, I solicited the assistance of Kirk, one of my new colleagues, to help me in 'pulling' the pallet to the front.

Closing the Gap

LEADERSHIP TIP 3:

Listen intently, write down important facts or details, and communicate clearly.

Unknown to me at the time, if you do not put the pallet jack fully into the pallet, when you pump the handle, you simply spread the pallet jack between the upper and lower boards of the pallet.

The result is instead of rolling the pallet on the pallet jack wheels, if you are able to move the pallet, it is literally just being dragged. This is exactly what we did. We dragged a pallet of merchandise across the brand new, freshly waxed linoleum tile floor.

It wasn't until we reached the front of the store that we realized what we had done. By that time, it was too late. There were scratches and scuff marks covering our entire path. When I saw them, I just knew that I'd be fired.

Although terrified of the consequences, I went to Ron and told him what we had done. The look on Ron's face when he saw what we had done conveyed his disappointment and anger. To his credit, he took a few moments to collect (*and likely filter*) his thoughts before telling us to take a break and then get back to it, we had lots of work to do to get the store opened on time.

The grace he showed us was truly unexpected and had a lasting impact. Besides making me work even harder, it also built loyalty to both him and the company.

...and the Lessons Learned:

- ### INTENT MATTERS.
  In this case, we made a significant mistake, however our intent was to do a good job. While not always possible to overlook a mistake, a person's intent should be considered (*when done righteously*) and grace extended whenever possible when no malicious intent or cause is determined.

- ### YOU SHOULDN'T MAKE DISCIPLINARY DECISIONS WHEN YOU'RE ANGRY.
  This may be simple, however all too often leaders will react and issue disciplinary actions out of anger versus reason. These rash actions often lead to decision reversals or regrets.

  This has been a leadership principle for me (*albeit I have not been perfect with adherence*) ever since that day, looking down at the scratched floor.

  Had the store manager fired me in his anger, while probably justified, he would have ended after a few weeks, the employment of someone who went on to work seven years for the company and left only after graduating from college.

Bridging the Gap
Performance Appraisal Methods

"People are your most important asset".

This adage or some variant began to increase in popularity when company leaders became '*enlightened*' in the second half of the last century.

During this time, many company leaders were forced to accept this new mindset as the conservative 1950s transitioned to the free-spirited 1960s and 1970s. Front-line company leaders resented the difficulty this new mindset brought to *'getting the job done'*.

In some form, this resentment has persisted over time and is still present in many companies. Therefore, it's no wonder that many of the basic personnel concepts associated with the *'enlightenment'* have been stagnated and disregarded for literally decades.

Employee performance appraisals are one of these personnel concepts.

What should be one of a leader's most important jobs is often a dreaded, low-priority, must do task that is given minimal effort.

If this describes you, what a lost opportunity!

In contrast, truly *'enlightened'* leaders (*hopefully you fall into this category*) view employee performance appraisals are a powerful tool. Furthermore, they understand that with candor and sincerity, appraisals can dramatically improve an employee's productivity and performance. Appraisals also help to release the untapped potential of your employees.

There are seven fundamental types of performance appraisals we will be discussing.

Figure 1

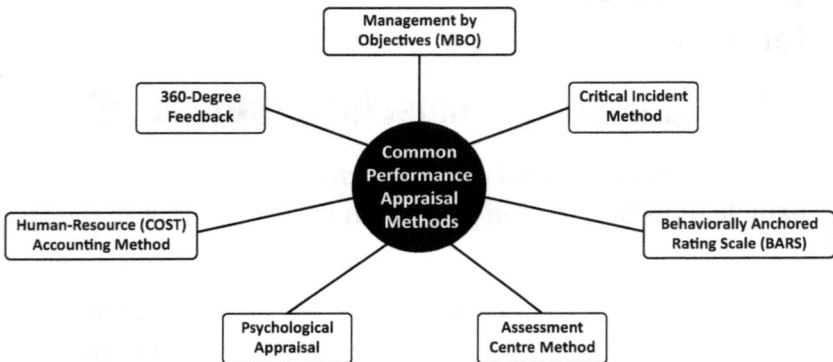

Chapter 4:

The Subordinate Romance

"Regardless of whether you work at an entry level position or as an executive, in most companies, exceptional performance will earn you political capital that will help to cover you."

– TIM MARSH

Contemplations:

- *Have you ever worked at a job where a supervisor was dating their subordinate? How did their relationship affect the work environment?*

- *Consider how nepotism (and in some cases family member employees) may have a similar impact on job results, performance, and satisfaction as a subordinate romance.*

Mind the Gap

"SO YOU TURNED OFF THE POWER, HUH...?"

The Story...

Location: Illinois

My last position at Target was as a cashier supervisor. At the time, I was going to college full-time and working full-time to pay my way. This did not leave a lot of time (*or money*) for dating.

The company's policy was clear that supervisors were prohibited from dating their subordinates. While I knew this, I also was aware of the steady stream of young women we hired as cashiers.

After a while, I gave into temptation and started a romantic relationship with one of these young ladies, Maddie.

Maddie and I dated on and off for a couple of years. As with many relationships between young people, ours lacked maturity and was full of emotion.

All of my friends in and out of work knew we were dating, yet we worked to keep the romance from the store managers. In hindsight, our efforts to keep the relationship on the down low were laughable. The romance became an open secret. I was able to pull off due to my strong work performance (*and likely management's reluctance to deal with the situation*).

Closing the Gap

LEADERSHIP TIP 4:

Encourage your people to contribute, be passionate, and embrace positivity.

As expected, when we were getting along well, things were fine at work. The problem (*and the primary reasons for company policies regarding workplace relationships*) was when things in the relationship were not so good.

Objectivity and impartiality are difficult in the best of scenarios, and all but impossible between romantic couples in the workplace.

While I tried to separate my personal and professional feelings (*which at the time I thought I had done well*), ultimately I couldn't. This impacted both of our work performances.

Eventually, it became apparent that we were in a relationship and management started to step up to their responsibility. Their off-hand questions and comments made it obvious that they knew and disapproved of the romance. As a result, Maddie decided to leave the company. Shortly afterward, our romance ended for good and we both moved on.

> **PERSONAL BACKSTORY:** I met my wife (*who was also one of my cashiers*) at Target. The difference though was that she was transferred to another department, so that we were not in a supervisor/subordinate relationship.
>
> At the time of this writing, we have been married over 22 years (*and yes, she is now the boss...*).

...and the Lessons Learned:

- **ROMANTIC WORKPLACE RELATIONSHIPS TRULY ARE A BAD IDEA.**
  Based not only on my experience but having seen many other workplace relationships, it is not possible for supervisors and subordinates in a romantic relationship to isolate their personal and professional behaviors.

- **WORKPLACE PERFORMANCE EARNS POLITICAL CAPITAL.**
  Regardless of whether you work in an entry level position or as an executive, in most companies, exceptional performance will earn you political capital (*sometimes also referred to as chits or brownie points*) that will help to cover you.

IMPORTANT: Keep in mind that there are some transgressions that cannot be overcome regardless of your performance.

Political capital is not finite (*you can't ask to use it*) but rather an unspoken workplace situational response.

Let me try to explain capital in a way in which you likely have experience in your personal life (*this is different from political capital earned at work*). Take for example, the friend who unintentionally says something offensive to you. More than likely you'll let the offending comment slide, whereas if it came from a stranger, you would have a different reaction. This is an example of the capital I'm talking about.

Bridging the Gap
Performance Appraisal Method: Management by Objectives (MBO)

Management by objectives (MBO) was popularized by Peter Drucker in the mid-1950s, although the concepts pre-date the Great Depression. It also happens to be the first performance appraisal system I experienced once entering the workforce after graduation.

Management by objective starts at the top of the company and proceeds downward to eventually involve each individual employee.

The five common steps to the management by objective process are:

1. **EVALUATE AND STATE THE COMPANY'S TARGETS AND OBJECTIVES.**

   These targets and objectives should incorporate your company's short and long term strategic directives. Additionally, they should adhere to your company's mission and values.

2. DEVELOP YOUR EMPLOYEES' OBJECTIVES IN LINE WITH YOUR COMPANY'S TARGETS AND OBJECTIVES.

Once your company's targets and objectives have been determined, your focus should be the development of your employees' objectives. The objectives should directly impact your company's ability to meet their overall targets and objectives.

3. DEVELOP INDIVIDUAL OBJECTIVES FOR EACH EMPLOYEE.

The individual objectives for your employees should align with the overall company strategic directives. These objectives are specific to the personal development of each individual employee. Giving your employees specific developmental objectives improves their competence, motivation, loyalty, performance, and results.

4. CONTINUOUS PERFORMANCE AND PROGRESS MONITORING.

You should continuously monitor your employee's objectives to ensure that they are achieving the desired company and individual results. By monitoring their progress, you can make the necessary adjustments to maximize their ability to successfully complete the objective.

5. EVALUATE, PROVIDE FEEDBACK, APPRAISE, AND REWARD.

Periodically, you should evaluate the employee's progress and schedule a time to provide them with feedback. These feedback sessions should be documented and occur several times during the rating period (*typically, objectives are given annually, and these periodic reviews are done quarterly*). At the end of the rating period, you should appraise each employees' results against the stated objective criteria. Employees that successfully achieve the desired results should be provided with agreed upon performance rewards.

When developing the objectives, it's common to use the **S.M.A.R.T.** *acronym:*

S – Specific.

Objectives must be specific to the desired result in order to prevent ambiguity. For example, rather than the objective being overly broad such as, "increase product quality rate", a specific objective would define the desired outcome, "increase quality rate of Product X to 99.25%".

M – Measurable.

A measurable objective is one that when an employee's result is evaluated against the stated criteria, the outcome is obvious as to whether the objective was achieved.

A – Acceptable/Achievable.

An acceptable objective is one that both management and the employee agree is achievable. In many cases, unachievable objectives would be those with either zero or 100% criteria, or ones that have numerous "switch criteria" that have to be turned on in order to meet the objective.

R – Realistic.

A realistic objective is one that is possible (albeit challenging) given the tools and resources available to the employee. Factors outside of the control of the employee are also considered.

T – Time Bound or Based.

A time bound or based objective is one that has a defined timeframe in which the result must be achieved. Objectives shouldn't be assumed to be time bound by the end of the evaluation period unless specifically noted. The

"increase product quality rate of Product X to 99.25%" should also have a time component, such as "within the next 180 days".

Proponents of management by objective believe it improves employee motivation while simultaneously improving communication between leadership and employees. It also helps to align individual efforts with the company's stated targets and objectives.

Critics of management by objective believe it focuses on individual goal setting in order to achieve specific objectives rather than the development of systematic plans to achieve broader company objectives.

Furthermore, critics claim that in order to achieve objectives, employees may make compromises (*including safety, quality, and profitability*) or take shortcuts.

Personally, I have had both good and bad experiences with the management by objective performance evaluation method. In both cases, it wasn't the method per se that worked or didn't, but rather the underlying leadership that made the difference.

The following is an example of a case in which this evaluation method didn't work. Our objective (*and bonus*) period went from January to December. We didn't get our objectives until March, and by that time some of the objectives were already unable to be achieved (*so in essence they were dead on arrival*). Obviously, this was a demotivator.

In the case where it work well, we were given objectives along with stretch goals. We all worked well that year and achieved great progress. At the end of the year, we met our objectives and our stretch goals, and we were all rewarded for it. You better believe we were ready to hit the ground running the next year.

Chapter 5:

Competence Failure

"Leaders who fail to continually develop their people's competence allow the short-sided cost and time saving benefits to supersede the long-term competitive advantages of having a competent workforce."

– TIM MARSH

Contemplations:

- *Think about a time you worked with an incompetent colleague or supervisor. Why were they incompetent? How did their incompetency affect your performance and overall results?*

- *Have you resigned only to then be offered a counteroffer? Why do you think the company was willing to do this when you resigned, but not proactively before?*

HE MANAGES A MULTI-BILLION DOLLAR BUSINESS YET STILL MAKES TIME TO APPROVE 50¢ AN HOUR RAISES.

The Story...
Location: West Virginia

I was starting a new area manager role during yet another industry downturn. This was not my first (*and unfortunately wouldn't be my last*) downturn. As a result, I knew my new leadership team and I had to rush to understand the business impact, estimate the price bottom, and predict the duration of the downturn. In these cases, the first company to understand and then act is often in the best position to weather the storm.

Each time I'd seen a downturn, the industry underwent significant changes. Large numbers of people lost their jobs while companies were forced to improve efficiencies. Ultimately, the industry always moved towards becoming more streamlined.

In many ways, industry downturns are similar to a phoenix; it burns down the old operating methods and new ways of operating rise from the ashes.

I have always been more successful having a smaller team with high quality people rather than a larger team with mixed quality people. High quality team members don't want to work with underperforming team members.

After evaluating the people in my new organization, I realized there was significant room for improvement in training and competency. Historically, these improvements are done to increase competitiveness. In a downturn, they are vital to survival.

Our business relied on field operators. They were typically high school educated, hard-working people. Prior to my arrival, little effort had been made to increase the competency of these operators for years, if not decades. As a result, most had tons of seniority with little technical knowledge.

One of the ways that I planned to increase the operator's knowledge was by conducting training. By completing the training, my operators not only increased their contribution to the company, but also qualified for a promotion. I arranged for an operator trainer to fly from Texas to West Virginia in order to conduct the senior operator school.

LEADERSHIP TIP 5:

Surround yourself with people who are smarter than you and then let the team have the credit for victories.

The guys were great. Although we literally had to help some work a calculator, they all passed the class. Their hard work and dedication to learn the material and pass the tests was an inspiration to all of us.

I was proud to put through their promotion paperwork and pay raise adjustment forms to move them from Operator to Senior Operator.

A few days later, I got a call from Katie, the human resources manager for our product line. She informed me that Fred, the vice president for all product lines, had denied the raises.

I was shocked.

Why was the person running a three billion dollar business in the midst of a serious industry downturn spending time approving hourly employee pay raises?

Her response floored me. "He has to approve all raises," she said. At the time, there were thousands of employees reporting to Fred.

All I could think was that we are in a downturn and all of the other product line areas' profits were negative, and you have nothing better to do. I couldn't understand why he was interfering in my business when I had clearly shown the ability to maintain profitability.

> **PERSONAL BACKSTORY:** I knew Fred and had been in many meetings with him. He was a long time company employee who had grown up in the highly profitable, non-technical side of the business. Having started out as a shop worker, he liked to tell people that he graduated from the "University of the Slab" (*the slab is another name for the shop floor*).
>
> He was close friends with the CEO, and that had likely been the reason he had been elevated several levels higher than I felt he deserved.
>
> My initial reservations came the first time I saw how he always parked across the best two parking spots in the parking garage. This and essentially the whole manner in which he operated reeked of *"look at me, I am important"*.
>
> In actuality, he was all show and no substance. All I saw was an empty suit, in way over his head. As is common with many weak leaders, he had surrounded himself with subordinates who bolstered his ego and never challenged or exposed his incompetence.
>
> As a result, when he retired, any of the slate of replacement candidates in his team would perpetuate his same issues.

The fact is, his actions were counterproductive in two ways. First, he hindered my ability to generate more revenue. Second, they demotivated both me and my people.

It was unbelievable…! He and his successors' actions (*which led to my loss of faith in the company leadership*) prompted me to be open to calls I often received from recruiters. Soon afterwards, when a recruiter called with another opportunity, I accepted it and left the leadership (*not the company*).

...and the Lessons Learned:

- **IN CRISIS SITUATIONS, ACTION SHOULDN'T BE MISTAKEN FOR LEADERSHIP.**
Often when a crisis occurs, regardless of the cause, leaders feel the need to do something. When this need is accompanied by a profound lack of understanding as to what action needs to be taken, weak leaders will start focusing on the minutia in order to show others they are acting. Strong leaders have the ability to pause and reflect as long as necessary to take decisive and meaningful action. In the situation described, I felt that rather than approving minimal employee raises, the VP should have focused on identifying actions he could take to help the other areas.

- **EMPLOYEE COMPETENCE IS A COMPETITIVE ADVANTAGE.**
Leaders who fail to continually develop their people's competence (*even in a downturn or slow growth period*) allow the short-sided cost and time saving benefits to supersede the long-term competitive advantages of having a competent workforce. These same leaders will often fail to understand the cause for their decreased competitiveness.

- **EMPLOYEES OFTEN LEAVE LEADERS, NOT THE COMPANY.**
It is not enough for a company's leadership to only focus on their own actions. They must also ensure that employees throughout the organization act in accordance with the company's values and ethics. Employees are often loyal to a company. However, they ultimately decide to leave a company because of a bad supervisor (*or poor leadership in the company hierarchy*). As in my case, the CEO made a bad decision by promoting his friend far beyond his capability and the result was that poor leaders propagated throughout his organization and many talented employees exited the company.

Bridging the Gap
Performance Appraisal Method: Critical Incident Method

The critical incident method, also known as the critical incident technique, was popularized in the mid-1950s. It utilizes a set of procedures to collect, observe, and analyze your employee's behavior during specific events (*critical incidents*). This process occurs with both favorable (*effective, good, positive*) behavior and unfavorable (*ineffective, bad, negative*) behavior.

The five-stages of the critical incident method are:

1. **Establish Intent.**

    This is essentially a general statement of the objectives to be accomplished throughout the process of collecting, observing, and analyzing the employee's behavior.

2. **Planning and Conditions.**

    These define the critical incidents to be observed and specifies who will conduct the observations (*whether by name, job title, position level, etc.*).

3. **Collecting Information.**

    This defines the data to be gathered for each critical incident as well as the method or methods used for collection of the information (*individual or group interviews, forms or questionnaires, etc.*).

4. **Information Analysis.**

    This step involves the analysis, classification, categorization, and subsequent use of the behavioral and situational data collected.

5. **Evaluation and Feedback.**

    In this step, all the data and analyses are interpreted

to determine root causes, motivating factors, and solutions. Once interpreted, the outcome is reported and feedback is given (*in addition to individual feedback, leaders should address any systemic issues leading to the behavior, whether favorable or unfavorable*).

The method is focused on your employee's development and coaching. Therefore, a rating isn't typically assigned to each critical incident (*although in some instances they may be coupled with an evaluative rating system*). Instead, at the end of the rating period, you make a cumulative review of all of the critical incidents and use this in the evaluation process.

Generally, you should record critical incidents immediately following the behavior. Any significant delay could result in unintentional inaccuracy and loss of crucial details.

The use of the critical incident method is more demanding on you than other performance evaluation methods. This has both positive and negative implications.

An advantage of this method is the process allows you to give regular feedback throughout the rating period. For favorable behaviors, your employees receive appreciation which translates into better morale, motivation, and performance. For unfavorable behaviors, you have the opportunity to develop and coach your employees sooner than if the behavior (*performance*) was only reviewed at the end of the rating period. Another advantage is that this method allows you to focus on multiple, isolated (*or one off*) events throughout the review period that may not be captured with other appraisal methods that focus only on common or overall results. It's often these type of events that differentiate your employees.

A disadvantage of this method is that you may delay or forego documenting critical incidents due to your workload (*or focus only on documenting the unfavorable behaviors as the priority*). As a result, some leaders (*hopefully not you in most cases*) have their employees document their own critical incidents (*in this scenario, employees tend to focus only on documenting favorable behaviors*). Ultimately, it's your responsibility to record the critical incidents. Delegating this responsibility to your employees only works if you give thorough directions to your employees with regard to which critical events to document (*both favorable and unfavorable*) and then review the documentation for accuracy and content. Another disadvantage to this method is bias on your part (*this is not a criticism; we all have biases*). This bias may be unintentional (*as in the case where you prioritize negative events due to timing and workload*) or intentional due to a variety of reasons (*discrimination, previous conflict, or simply your negative feelings about an employee*).

The critical incident method for employee performance evaluation is best suited for a company with a culture of execution and candor.

In this environment, the method will see maximum results for both the employees and the company.

"Continuous improvement is better than delayed perfection."

– MARK TWAIN

Chapter 6:

The Performance Bar

"When you are flexible with the path to performance, you can set the bar much higher."

– Tim Marsh

Contemplations:

- *Have you ever accidentally 'put your foot in your mouth' with a colleague or your supervisor? How was the situation handled? Did it have a long-term impact on your working relationship?*

- *Think of a time when internal competition was having a negative impact. Was the competition encouraged? What was the effect on the collegial relationships? Did leadership put an end to the internal competition?*

Mind the Gap

HE'S DONE IT WRONG SO LONG HE THINKS IT'S RIGHT.

The Story...
Location: Various

PERSONAL BACKSTORY: Less than a month into my first job out of college, I was in an outside sitting area near Tulsa, Oklahoma, awaiting my turn at the company's driver training school. There were two others there, Bernie and Jerry. They turned out to be instructors for the upcoming ten-week training course I was scheduled to attend later that month.

Unfortunately for me, I did not know they were instructors at the time. We started chatting, just to pass the time, and the topic of my upcoming training course came up. "What do you think about going to that course?" they asked. I responded that I was excited to attend.

Then (*in a moment that I now find funny, although there were times when I felt differently*) I went on to say something to the effect of "*although I heard the instructors are all pricks*". To their credit, they never let on as to who they were.

After completing my pre-school training period (*and the driver training course*), I showed up at the training center in Shreveport. As we sat down for an introductory meeting with the instructors and students, Bernie and Jerry walked out. They both had big smiles on their face as they pointed at me and nodded their heads. I was devastated. To their credit, they were good-natured about the whole thing, although I wasn't able to live down my comment during the training.

The training was tough. When I say tough, I mean tough. I had just completed my degree in engineering and that was nothing compared to this.

The rules were clear. The consequences were well laid out. There would be quizzes almost daily along with simulated wellsite exercises and tests. Get below a 70 on more than two and you would be terminated. Be late to class more than twice and you would be terminated. I felt like we were about to walk a high wire with no net.

The competition between the students was intense. The other students in the group were cutthroat and unwilling to help. For the longest time, the top 10 students were within three tenths of a percentage point of each other. Luckily, I was in that group.

As it turns out, being on time to class became the biggest struggle. All the students were sharing apartments several miles from the training center. My fiancé was driving my car at the time so I had to catch a ride to class everyday with my roommate. He was perpetually running late, and the situation was exacerbated by the seemingly endless traffic on the two-lane road leading to the training center.

I still have vivid memories of listening to Twisted Sister's *"We're Not Going to Take It"* at deafening levels while riding in his tiny car past stopped traffic and through the grass ditch in order to get to class on time. After ten weeks, I graduated from the course and continued on with my career.

PERSONAL BACKSTORY: My wife and I were married on September 11, 1998, the same day I graduated from the training course.

Unfortunately, a number of my colleagues did not make it through the course. My roommate quit on the last day of class. He'd wanted to prove to himself that he could pass the course, but he no longer wanted to work for the company.

Later in my career, I had the opportunity to be a tutor for a short time at the company's Venezuela training center. The class before I arrived had lost 50% of the students. While my time in Venezuela was cut short by a worker's strike (*we were locked in the compound with the military protecting us; an interesting story in itself but alas for another time*), I came to understand that many of the students failing the training course were smart, high-potential engineers that would have been great assets to the company. At that time however, the oilfield was booming. Fixing the problem with attrition at the training centers was not on the agenda.

When I returned to the United States and resumed my senior field engineer position, the shortage of new engineers grew more desperate. As a result, the company lowered the standards at the training centers. This meant that some students who scored below 70 percent now passed the training.

LEADERSHIP TIP 6:

Demand integrity from yourself and others, tell the truth, and trust your team.

One of these students, Andy, was a junior field engineer from my district. Upon his return, the district manager came to me and said, "You're the biggest a**hole so I'm assigning him to you.". I hoped this comment was intended as a joke and that he assigned him to me because I had the most seniority and competence. Regardless, it was up to me to train and prepare Andy to breakout as a field engineer (*Breakout was an eight-hour oral examination that covered all aspects of the job. Upon successful completion, the junior field engineer was promoted to field engineer. Field engineers were able to perform jobs and earn job bonus without having a training engineer on location*).

Training Andy proved to be tough. I could see why his grades were so low at the training center. Andy was stubborn. This complicated matters as my patience was virtually non-existent. Andy (*though extremely smart and dedicated*) was a slow learner. However, once he grasped a concept, the knowledge was rock solid.

Andy's training involved a lot of what I referred to as 'tough love lessons'. One such lesson I can remember occurred when I sent him to the rig floor to get the drilling mud information. He came back with everything but the viscosity from the mud report. When I questioned him, he told me it wasn't on the report.

I asked him how many times we had gotten the mud data that the viscosity hadn't been on the report (*we had caught dozens of jobs together by that point*). He admitted that it had been there every other time. After arguing, I told him I would go get the viscosity.

I went to the doghouse (*the doghouse is what they call the small office located on the drilling rig floor*) and sure enough, I found the viscosity data. When I returned, Andy asked if I'd found it. When I said yes, he asked me what it was, so he could enter it into the computer. I refused to give it to him. Instead, I told him to get up to the rig floor and find it himself. On the second trip, he did.

Another 'tough love lesson' I taught Andy occurred when he had to wade into the drilling mud pit to retrieve copies of paper logs.

Our older wireline trucks had a large main door on the passenger side that everyone entered through normally. There was also a small escape door on the driver's side in case the main door was inaccessible during an emergency. There was a small bench and counter near the door that was convenient to put offset paper logs to look at while acquiring data.

It wasn't uncommon to open the small door. Whether you were needing to talk to the crew on that side of the wireline truck or to let in some fresh air, it was convenient. The challenge was that if that door were open and someone opened the main door, the crosswind would blow things out of the truck.

I had warned Andy of this possibility. I told him that if he were going to open the small door to make sure there weren't any logs on the bench or counter that could blow out. I had learned this lesson myself when I was younger. I was trying to keep him from repeating my mistake.

He did. When the main door opened one day, the paper logs on the counter blew out of the wireline truck into the drilling mud pit. At first, he didn't believe me when I told him to go get them. When he finally understood I was serious, I'm sure he was glad he brought a 3 Day Bag with extra clothes and wet wipes, as I had recommended.

PERSONAL BACKSTORY: When working in the field, I recommended that everyone on the crew always carry what I called a '3 Day Bag', with enough supplies to live on location for three days. Besides clothes and toiletries (*including toilet paper*), I recommended bringing non-perishable food, water bottles, books, and wet wipes (*for a 'wellsite bath'*).

I learned this lesson when I was a junior field engineer. One day, I went out on a routine job that should have ended within a few hours. That morning before the job, I had asked one of the operators if we had food in the wireline truck. He said we did so I didn't stop at the store for anything on the way to the wellsite.

Let's just say that powdered cup of soup and microwave popcorn are not my idea of 'food'. To complicate matters, the job was extended, and we were stuck on location for several days. After several days of eating nothing but powdered soup and microwave popcorn, I vowed to never go on another wellsite unprepared again.

Eventually, Andy did break out as a field engineer. He was competent and did a good job for a number of years. Ultimately, he decided to leave the company and grow his career with a major international oil company.

...and the Lessons Learned:

- ### WHEN THERE ARE SYSTEMATIC FAILURES, DON'T FORGET TO LOOK INSIDE THE COMPANY FOR THE CAUSE.

  The company had spent much time and money developing and implementing an excellent recruiting and training program. Even with the highest quality people (*these students were all college graduates from some of the best universities around the world, and most of them had engineering degrees*), all of these efforts were thwarted by the lack of preparation.

  Besides the loss of thousands of dollars and countless hours of time, each students' failure at the training center ultimately reflected on a bigger issue, which was the company's inability to identify and address the root causes.

- ### LACK OF PREPARATION CAN UNDERMINE HIGH PERFORMANCE.

  Fortunately, the company did eventually take action to identify and address the root causes. Accepting part of the responsibility for the students' failures, the company began working on and eventually implemented a program to better prepare the students for their time at the training center. The result was a significant drop in the number of students failing the training center.

  This reduction resulted in less employee attrition, increased recruitment efficiency, and significant reduction in overall training costs. All in all, a win-win for both the company and the students.

- ### SET THE BAR HIGH, BUT BE FLEXIBLE.

  I encourage you to set the bar high when if comes to your expectations. In fact, I recommend setting it higher than you are comfortable. Why? Flexibility. When you are flexible with the path to performance, you can set the bar much higher. On the contrary, when you're too rigidity in the path to the expected level of performance, you can stagnate, demoralize, and derail your efforts.

Keep in mind that one-size-fits-all approaches, whether for performance or any other evaluation area, are the easier paths to take, however they often fail to accommodate non-tradition paths for performance.

Bridging the Gap

Performance Appraisal Method: Behaviorally Anchored Rating Scale (BARS)

The Behaviorally Anchored Rating Scale (BARS) is a scale used to measure your employees' performance. Developed in the middle of the last century, it uses methods such as critical incident techniques to develop comprehensive and specific behavioral task patterns. These are then used to rate your employees (*while the patterns may be specific to each employee, they often apply to multiple employees within similar roles*).

It is critical during development that leaders understand each of the employee's (or job position's) essential tasks along with the favorable and unfavorable behaviors associated with each.

One these tasks and behaviors are understood, the behaviorally anchored scale can be developed. It is usually a vertical scale with high rating point range from 5 to 9. Through the scale range, it gives behavioral examples of poor, moderate and good behavior or performance.

The BARS performance appraisal method is extremely specific to an employee (*or job position*) which gives you the ability to provide more concise feedback. This differs from basic rating scales that gives a more subjective performance rating.

There are numerous advantages to use of BARS:

- **Employees are rated by specific and concise individualized scale criteria that are easily understood by both the employee and leaders.**

- **Each scale rating has a very comprehensive example statement (*this makes evaluating the employee's performance less confusing*).**

- **The BARS employee appraisal process is fair and unbiased, as it is focused exclusively on the employee's own behavior.**

- **The behavioral anchor scale has concise and specific performance expectations. This gives employees landmarks to work towards in order to improve their performance and results.**

- **BARS maximizes employee results and performance as each behaviorally anchored scale is uniquely developed for an individual employee or job position.**

While there are numerous advantages to BARS, there are also some disadvantages that must be considered:

- **While being specific and individualized is an advantage, it comes at a financial cost. Depending on the company size (*and the number and variety of job positions*), this cost may be prohibitive for implementing BARS.**

- In addition to the financial cost, the specification and individualization also requires a substantial amount of the leaders' time.

- Managers must be motivated and highly involved, these appraisals require detailed information about employees.

- Some employees have job positions with numerous job expectations. For these employees (*and job positions*) it is not realistic or feasible to have scales for each expectation.

- In scales where the differentiation between ratings is minimal, it is possible for bias and rating inconsistencies to be introduced into the performance appraisals.

"In many cases, the best team decision will not be a consensus decision."

– Tim Marsh

Mind the Gap:
Leadership Basics I

Giving Graft to Your Employees

There are numerous benefits to giving company branded graft to your employees. It can increase fellowship when everyone on the team is wearing or has the same item (*such as matching t-shirts or hats*). Graft can also be a reward for healthy internal competition. An additional benefit with giving graft to employees is external sales and marketing efforts (*i.e. wearing company branded attire*).

Micromanagement

Micromanaging is when a leader attempts to manage or control every aspect or detail of the work assigned to their subordinates.

Although common around the world, micromanagement has a negative impact on employees' performance and morale. Regardless of intent, if you micromanage your employees, you risk conveying a lack of trust in their competency, integrity, or both.

Common micromanaging actions include requesting subordinates to BCC (*blind carbon copy*) you on their emails, eavesdropping on conversations, hovering in workspaces, and excessive questioning.

Stretch Objectives

While developing employee performance objectives, consider assigning them stretch objectives. These may range from additional objectives, stretching already agreed upon objective targets, or both.

These objectives stretch your employees to achieve greater results. Therefore, the upside for achieving them should reflect the accomplishment.

There shouldn't however, be a downside for attempting but not achieving the stretch objectives.

Explaining the 'Why' of Your Decisions

As a leader, it is your prerogative to make decisions and implement them via directives to your employees. It is expected that they will take these directives and enact them. The question is whether this is the best technique to lead your team?

There is a significant distinction between choosing to explain the 'why' to your employees versus being questioned 'why'. Consider how explaining your decision criteria and thought process may help them to better understand your decisions.

Explaining the 'why' of your decisions to your employees is a testament of your trust and confidence. It also demonstrates your respect for their thoughts and opinions.

These serve to improve your employees' decision buy-in, job performance, and overall results.

Creating a Productive Work Environment

Your employees' work environment influences their mood and performance. This in turn affects the ability for them to focus on assignments along with their overall health and happiness.

Consider the impact of the following on your work environment:

- Air temperature (comfortable vs. uncomfortable)
- Lighting (natural vs. artificial)
- Furniture and décor (updated vs. drab and dated)
- Work area (cubicles vs. offices)
- Plants (artificial vs. live)
- Drinks (sodas vs. healthy drinks… *and coffee!*)
- Noise (ambient vs. music)
- Wall color (institutional vs. vibrant colors)

These are just a few environmental factors that impact your employees.

What can be done to improve your work environment?

Keep in mind that environmental upgrades are an investment in your employees' job performance and results.

Hearing but Not Listening

There is a difference between hearing and actively listening to what is said. While the distinction may be subtle, it is extremely important. Active listening conveys your understanding of what your employee is saying while acknowledging and accepting their feelings.

In order to actively listen, you must attempt to forego any personal agenda, biases, or pre-judgments and focus only on what is being said. After active listening, you should respond by mirroring back to them what you heard. This allows the employee to know you understood what they said.

Employee Appreciation

A troublesome fact is that many leaders fail to understand the power of showing appreciation to their employees. The reasons range from ignorance to attitude to indifference. Remarkably, some managers still have the misguided notion that an employees' paycheck is the only appreciation required. Would you want to work for one of these people? *I doubt it.*

Appreciation is a simple act, yet it has become far less common in the fast paced, disconnected world today. At work (*and also at home*), receiving appreciation promotes self-worth, motivation, and uplifting feelings about yourself. In addition to the positive feelings when you receive appreciation, when you give honest and sincere appreciation, you also enjoy many of these same positive feelings.

Here is an alarming revelation. Your employees are likely receiving less appreciation than you think. Consider this, when was the last time you showed them some appreciation? When is the last time you were shown appreciation? Whether from those who think they give more than they do, to those who think appreciation only comes in the form of a paycheck, there is usually vast room for improvement.

You should encourage all of your employees to provide frequent honest and sincere appreciation. Keep in mind, reward and recognition initiatives rolled out by your company, while technically appreciation, aren't the same as in-person, one-on-one appreciation.

The best approach for creating a culture of appreciation is from top-down leading by example in an environment that encourages all employees to genuinely care about their fellow employees.

Non-Performing Employees

We have all worked with an underperforming co-worker, leader, or subordinate. Usually there's at least one contributing factor leading to them still being employed. These vary from long tenure with the company to simply being a really nice person.

Regardless, these under performers tend to linger in many companies because leaders don't want to manage the situation. Yes, these are tough situations (*especially with long-term and really friendly employees*) but this is why performance management systems are essential. They not only provide guidelines to manage performance, but also have mechanisms to prevent underperformers from lingering with the company.

One of the most important reasons for addressing underperforming employees is the negative impact that they have on your best performing employees. Highly-talented and skilled employees do not want to be burdened with underperformers.

Failure to address this problem will undoubtedly have detrimental consequences. These include higher employee attrition and frustration (*especially of high performing employees*) in addition to lower overall team performance.

"Never, never, never, never give up."

– WINSTON CHURCHILL

Chapter 7:

Inherent Conflict

"High quality people prefer working in a meritocracy free of distractions where they can be part of a team achieving maximum results."

– TIM MARSH

Contemplations:

- *Have you ever worked in an environment where your supervisor was rooting for you to fail? What was the cause? How did you work through this experience?*

- *Consider a time when a new venture succeeded beyond anyone's expectations. What were the factors leading to the success? Were the lessons learned? Were best practices from the success communicated to other areas of the company?*

"I SURE HOPE THIS IS AN OPEN BOOK TEST."

The Story...

Location: Texas

PROFESSIONAL BACKSTORY: Electric wireline is an oilfield service that uses a truck or offshore skid with a drum of steel cable with one or more insulated copper conductors to convey tools into a wellbore. The steel cable provides mechanical strength for the operation, and the copper conductors transmit power and data. In the scenario when the tools lowered into the well become stuck, it is typical to have a weak point at the connection of the cable and tools. This allows the stuck tools to be left in the well and the cable preserved.

When conducting wireline operations on a well with pressure, equipment is required for the wireline tools to be run in and out of the well without releasing the pressure and wellbore fluids. When the tools are brought to the surface, they are contained inside the lubricator (*which allows the well to be closed at the wellhead*). In these applications, it's required to perform "bump up" procedures. These are required because it is not possible to stop the drum in time when the tools reach the top of the lubricator to prevent unintentionally pulling out of the weak point.

Bump up procedures involve one or more operators holding down on the wireline as the tools approach surface. Our company policy was to start bumping up when the tools were 200 feet below the surface. When the tools bump up against the top of the lubricator, the tension increases and lifts up the wireline the operators are holding down. As long as the winch operator stops the winch before the wireline gets taught, the weak point won't break (*which is referred to as an unintentional pulled off or UPO*).

My wireline career started in Tyler, Texas as a junior field engineer. I was part of a test group of new hires that started degreed engineers in cased hole rather than open hole (*which had been the standard*).

As the only degreed engineer from this program operating a wireline truck in the district, there were conflicts between me and the other completion specialists who had worked their way through the ranks. Where my seniority with the company was mere months, all of theirs were years (*with most having 20 plus years of seniority*).

Closing the Gap

LEADERSHIP TIP 7:

Make calculated decisions, never stop improving, try new things, and encourage creativity.

The conflicts that occurred were predictable.

In addition to conflicts with the other completion specialists, my immediate supervisors (*who were previously completion specialists*) also took issue with me operating a truck with such little seniority, as they too had worked their way through the ranks.

Upon my breakout as a field engineer, I was not surprised to be given the wireline truck and tools in the worst condition and assigned the most inexperienced crew in the district.

Our combined seniority added up to a fraction of the average completion specialist crew. Despite our inexperience, our crew was successful in completing jobs. Most often, these were the worst jobs in the district. The better jobs (*the ones that had less work, higher bonuses, or both*) were assigned to the completion specialists.

My crew and I therefore cut our teeth on low bonus, heavy physical labor perforating jobs (*perforating is when explosive shape charges are used to make holes in pipe*). These jobs typically involved cranes, pressure control equipment, and heavy tool strings. Many days, we would make multiple runs, requiring my crew to bump up on each run. This was in addition to having to rig up a crane, pressure control equipment, and assemble the multiple tool strings.

One day my crew and I were on location doing yet another mundane job requiring seven heavy tool string runs. The heavier the tool string, the harder it is to bump up. On this job, my crew got progressively more tired throughout the day due to high outdoor temperatures and the large workload. By the last run, they were nearly worn out, and we still had to rig down all of the equipment. Therefore, on the last run in the hole, I decided that rather than making the crew bump up the last 200 feet, I would start at 50 feet to help reduce the effort required by the crew.

Having bumped up six times previously, I was confident at what depth the tools would bump up in the lubricator. As I was nearing the surface, something went wrong and the tools hung up before my crew had started to bump up. The result was that I unintentionally pulled out of the weak point. When this happened, the tool string fell to bottom, requiring a fishing job.

Once the district concluded the investigation, it was confirmed that I violated the company bump up policy (*we had been honest with what had happened*). As a result, I received a four-day suspension without pay. This in itself would not have been an issue as that was pretty standard, other than I had personally witnessed several other at-fault UPOs in the district. When these had occurred, they hadn't resulted in any disciplinary action. Although I don't know for sure, I suspect that these UPOs were covered up by the supervisors for their longtime friends (*the other completion specialists*). When I made a mistake, however, they definitely took the opportunity to issue consequences.

...and the Lessons Learned:

- **MANAGEMENT SUPPORT OF NEW COMPANY INITIATIVES MUST EXTEND FROM TOP TO BOTTOM.**

  There were a number of corporate objectives with the test group. The primary one was to increase the number of engineers in the US and Canadian operations that would spend more of their field career in cased hole.

  None of these objectives were communicated to the organization. This combined with a lack of visible corporate leadership commitment resulted in the entire initiative languishing. The attrition rate among the test group engineers was above average.

  A significant factor with the disconnect was corporate leadership's failure to understand or consider how the US and Canadian operations differed from those else-where in the world (*internationally, there were few completion specialists*).

  In contrast, most US and Canadian cased hole jobs were run by completion specialists who had worked their way through the ranks from field operators.

  In these operations, putting freshly hired, degreed engineers making higher salaries than the completion specialists to run the high-tech services (*which paid the highest bonus rates*) presented many challenges. Need-less to say, the initiative didn't work well.

  The challenges were exacerbated by district managers (*who were exclusively degreed engineers that started in open hole*) that were not directed as to desired utilization of the new engineers.

As a result, the district managers usually perpetuated the challenges by either disregarded the issues with the new cased hole engineers or sided with the majority of the district employees in their disdain for these engineers because of the disruptions they caused in their business.

- **CONSISTENCY WITH DISCIPLINE IS KEY TO GOOD RANK AND FILE ORDER.**
I was not looking to have my UPO covered up, however I did feel that management should have consistently applied disciplinary actions to all employees.

By their lack of consistency, they (*whether intentional or not*) undermined my faith and loyalty to the company while creating a work environment plagued with politics, cronyism, and favoritism.

It should go without saying that companies with politics, cronyism, and favoritism can't consistently attract and retain high quality people.

High quality people prefer working in a meritocracy where they are part of a high-performance team that achieves outstanding results.

Bridging the Gap
Performance Appraisal Method: Assessment Centre Method

For the purpose of evaluating performance, an assessment centre (*these were developed in Germany and later used extensively in England, so I will continue with 'centre' vs. 'center'*) is a location (*either onsite or offsite*) to evaluate an employee.

This evaluation is to determine the employee's performance within a position or potential for a new position.

At an assessment centre, trained evaluators observe, assess, and rank an employee's core functional abilities, job related characteristics, and future potential to perform new job duties.

Assessment centres may conduct a variety of activities depending on the desired outcome. These activities may include observed behavior based assessments, personality tests, exams (*IQ, general knowledge, specialized knowledge, etc.*), psychological tests, job simulations and role-playing activities.

Job simulations and role playing activities are used to evaluate candidates on behaviors and competency related to the most essential aspects of the job.

Assessment centres may use a group exercise (these typically involve a group of 8-10 employees) during the evaluation process.

Implementation guidelines for assessment centre method:

- Use critical incident technique or job analysis to ascertain the performance components

- Develop the performance metrics for each component

- Determine appropriate and relevant employee behavior for the assessment centre evaluation process

- Select which assessment centre methods are best suited to obtain the desired behavior information

- Identify and provide training to the assessors and reviewers

- Assess, collect, analyze, and record information for each employee

- Provide feedback, create development and improvement plans, and/or acknowledge (*and reward*) the employee.

There are several advantages to using an assessment centre (some of these extend beyond performance evaluation into other functions, such as recruiting):

- Widely considered to be a fair evaluation technique

- Improves equality and diversity among candidate selection

- Recognizes employee merit

- Improves success rate for candidate selection

- Assesses employee competency and performance

- Predicts employee's future job performance

- Promotes company brand

The disadvantages of using an assessment centre (again, some of these extend beyond performance evaluation):

- High cost compared to other evaluation methods

- Time-consuming (*especially for the company's top leadership*)

- Risk that the evaluators may demonstrate bias (*whether intentional or not*)

- Potential for candidates to not receive feedback

"There is little success where there is little laughter."

— ANDREW CARNEGIE

Chapter 8:

"Who's going to catch the job?"

"By actively managing change at lower organizational levels, many incidents can be averted and operating tasks improved."

– Tim Marsh

Contemplations:

- *Have you ever been in a situation where you thought doing the right thing may jeopardize your job? Was the threat from a single person or systematic throughout the company? How did you handle the situation?*

- *Recall a time in which you didn't have the proper equipment to perform a job task. How did you proceed? Were you able to complete the job? Did you or anyone else compromise your safety in order to get the job done?*

"THIS ISN'T WHAT I WAS THINKING WHEN
I SAID AN INSTRUMENT OF CHANGE."

The Story...

Location: Texas

PROFESSIONAL BACKSTORY: Perforating guns used in wireline are essentially long steel tubes filled with explosive shaped charges, detonating cord, electric wires, and a detonator.

They are run in a well on the end of wireline and detonated at a desired depth to punch holes in the steel casing and rock formation. This allows the fluid in the formation to enter the well to be produced.

We were loading out to do a perforating job for one of our best customers. The ten 4-1/2″ diameter, 20′ long perforating guns we were loading were heavy even with five people working together to lift them. The trailer that we were using to haul them to the wellsite was already loaded with other equipment we were taking with us for the job.

Closing ▷◁ the Gap

LEADERSHIP TIP 8:

Understand your leadership style, lead all generations, and share your vision with your people.

We were about to load the last gun when instead of just carrying it onto the trailer and dropping it in place like we had for the first nine guns, for some reason, we decided to change loading procedure. We decided that the first two guys would set their end down and then come around to help me and the two others set our end down.

The first end was set down, but instead of only two guys letting go, everyone let go but me. Suddenly, I had all of the weight of my end of the gun. With all the extra weight, I could feel the perforating gun start to slip through my hands. As I stepped back to reposition myself and get a better grip, I accidently stepped on another gun we had already loaded. The gun rolled and my ankle twisted. I lost my balance and fell to the floor. In the process, the falling gun landed on my left hand.

There wasn't immediate pain, even though a several hundred pound perforating gun fell several feet onto my hand. It was more of a numb, tingling sensation. I remember sitting on my butt and clutching my hand (*as my ankle was sprained too*).

One of my operators said, "Man, that had to hurt!". By that time, it did hurt. It hurt bad. Luckily, another operator pulled out his pocketknife, cut off my glove, and helped me to remove my wedding ring. My wedding ring (*a thick gold band*) was bent into an oval due to the impact. It didn't take long for my hand to start swelling.

I assumed my hand was broken. It was throbbing and the swelling was so bad that I thought my skin may actually split open. I knew I couldn't catch the job now, so I started thinking about who could. I called another engineer who was off-duty. He wasn't excited about coming in to do the job (*not only was it his day off, but this was a hard job with big guns*). He finally agreed, and I turned my attention to getting medical attention.

Once the situation had been handled, I called my supervisor to give him a status report. When I told him that I thought I had broken my hand, his response was, "Who's going to catch the job?" I informed him that I had already arranged for another engineer to catch the job. I also told him that I was going to call my wife to take me to the hospital.

It was a sign of the time in the oilfield that his first concern was catching the job, and somewhere down the list was my wellbeing.

In our district, we were divided into three-person crews (*an engineer and two operators*). When a job was completed, each crew member would receive a bonus. These job bonuses were a large part of our overall income. There weren't any spare employees, therefore if I had to take time off to recover, my two operators wouldn't be able to earn any job bonuses.

In those days, oilfield crews operated like family (*if one of your family members had a problem while you were on a job, someone from the shop would go to help them*). It wasn't uncommon for the crews to spend more time with each other than with their own families. Like I said, the oilfield was a much different place back then.

As it turns out, my hand wasn't broken, but it was severely crushed. The pain, bruising, and swelling were severe. Fortunately, the accident happened on a Friday, so I had a couple days to recover over the weekend. By Monday, my hand was still the size of a baseball catcher's mitt, but I was back at work nonetheless.

My crew and I worked together so we could still catch jobs. It took several weeks, but we made it through the recovery process together.

In those days, employees that missed work due to an injury tended to get laid off or fired. It seemed to be one of the unspoken rules of the oilfield before things started changing.

...and the Lessons Learned:

- **PROMOTE LEADERS WHOSE CORE VALUES PRIORITIZE PEOPLE OVER REVENUE.**
  While this may seem simplistic and obvious, people's core values may not be easy to evaluate. Most leaders understand that the company wants them to respect and value their people. As a result, some work to instill this as a core value, while others will adopt a superficial persona in line with the company's desires.

  Given enough time, the superficial persona leaders will ultimately fail. Why? The simple answer is that when a challenging situation or crisis arises, they will naturally migrate towards action in line with their true core values. At that point, any false persona on the leader's part will become obvious to everyone.

This is the case with my supervisor in the example I described. When he heard of the incident, his first reaction was to worry about catching the job (*which was the priority from his perspective*). By the time he remembered to be concerned about me, his superficial persona of valuing people was quite obvious to all.

- ### EMBRACE MANAGEMENT OF CHANGE FROM BOTTOM UP.

  In many companies, employees usually don't understand or use management of change (MOC). This is usually because MOC efforts are administered from the top down, and employees are neither required nor asked to participate significantly beyond implementing the changes given to them. When operating from the top down, MOC activities are often subject to only major company changes due to the time limitations of leadership.

In companies that practice bottom up MOC, the change efforts are administered as close to the changed standard, process, or procedure as possible. This method allows those employees (*or other stakeholders*) most impacted by the change to participate in the efforts. In bottom up MOC operations, change criteria (*whether cost, time, or other thresholds*) ensure the proper level of leadership administers the MOC efforts.

By actively managing change at lower organizational levels, many incidents can be averted and operating tasks improved.

There are significant long-term benefits for using MOC techniques to prevent minor incidents or improve basic tasks (*whether quality, safety, financial, etc.*). These include being able to utilize MOC more efficiently for larger company changes, as well as the ability to better mitigate more serious incidents.

Bridging the Gap

Performance Appraisal Method: Psychological Appraisal

Psychological appraisals are beneficial for determining the untapped potential of your employees. This performance appraisal method concentrates on analyzing your employee's future potential rather than their historical performance.

When conducting a psychological appraisal, a qualified psychologist works with your employee to evaluate and analyze seven performance components.

These components include:

1. **Interpersonal relationship skills**
2. **Cognitive competence**
3. **Intellect (IQ)**
4. **Leadership skills**
5. **Personality traits**
6. **Emotional quotient**
7. **Future position skills**

A psychologist evaluation and analysis process typically includes in-depth interviews, psychological tests, individual discussions, etc. It's usually a time-consuming and complex process that relies heavily on the quality of the psychologist.

There are several advantages of psychological appraisals:

- Obtains information about both employee performance and future potential

- Lower cost and time intensive compared with other performance appraisal methods (*this appears as both an advantage and disadvantage as this method is mid-range for cost and time)*

- Works well to obtain information about performance and future potential from introverted employees

Psychological appraisals have several common failure causes and disadvantages:

- Lack of proper training

- Insufficient psychological professionals to administer

- Employee anxiety or nervousness affecting results

- More costly and time-consuming compared with other performance appraisal methods

"Retention efforts that focus on an employee's career development and advancement are most effective as they simultaneously benefit them and the company."

– TIM MARSH

Chapter 9:

When a Positive Turns Negative

"When you regularly provide appreciation, it has a positive impact on your employee's mood and improves their overall outlook and engagement."

– Tim Marsh

Contemplations:

- *Recall a time at work when something you thought was going to be a positive turned out to be a negative. What happened to change the outcome? How did the experience affect your job performance, satisfaction, and overall results?*

- *Have you ever worked where you felt your contributions were underappreciated? How did this affect your job results, performance, and satisfaction? What happened to resolve the matter?*

"THIS ISN'T THE EMPLOYEE RETENTION PROGRAM I HAD ENVISIONED."

The Story...

Location: Oklahoma

I had been a field engineer for about a year, and I was preparing to take my senior field engineer exam. Besides meeting the seniority requirement, I had to obtain enough proficiency and aptitude points in our progression program to qualify to take the exam.

Successfully completing the exam would bring a raise. In addition, it would bring me one step closer to becoming a general field engineer. Like the field engineer breakout exam, it would be an eight-hour oral exam that my manager and I would travel to Oklahoma City to complete.

PERSONAL BACKSTORY: I could feel the tension in the air when I arrived at the division office to take the exam. Come to find out, one of the employees in our district had complained to the division office about excessive drinking at the shop and the overflowing beer cans in the gun shop's trash cans.

While it may seem crazy today, back then it was not uncommon to have gun loading parties (*although I suspect they still occur*). They usually happened when crews were preparing for large perforating jobs. The parties typically involved drinking beer while loading explosives into perforating guns.

Needless to say, my manager was not happy about being there to discuss the issue in person with the division manager. I was not happy that everyone was upset, as I thought that would really not help me with the exam.

I was relieved once the exam started and contrary to what I'd expected, the gun loading party issue didn't have any effect. Eight hours is a long time to give presentations and answer questions. As a former introvert, I must admit that these breakout exams helped me to overcome any fears of public speaking (*which was one of the purposes*).

After we finished the exam and everyone was debriefed, the division manager, Tommy, asked me to come into his office. I was taken aback as we were about to leave for dinner. I couldn't think of why he would want a private meeting.

The conversation started with Tommy saying that what we would be discussing was private and I could not discuss it even with my manager. At first, I thought it had to do with the gun loading parties but I quickly realized it was much better. He was awarding me stock options. The award wasn't huge but I was super excited nonetheless.

He also talked with me about being on the high-potential list. Wow...! That finally explained why I had been given so many 'extra' tasks since I broke out. I could not believe that all of my hard work was starting to pay off.

My stock options were intended to be a retention incentive, so they took time to become vested. During this vesting time period, the company made a large acquisition that the stock market didn't like. The stock price dropped significantly.

Closing ▶◀ the Gap

LEADERSHIP TIP 9:

Stay curious, know when to ask questions, and let the best ideas win.

My options were so far underwater that I could never see myself making a penny with them (*and ultimately, I never did*). The company didn't make any efforts to address that they were now worthless. Thus, their retention efforts had a neutral impact at best, but in most cases they had a negative impact on those affected.

...and the Lessons Learned:

- **FEEDBACK SHOULDN'T BE RESERVED ONLY FOR POOR PERFORMANCE.**
  When you regularly provide appreciation, it has a positive impact on your employee's attitude and improves their overall engagement.

  You have likely heard the adage that "the squeaky wheel gets the grease". All too often, this is the case with poor performing employees.

  You're missing tremendous opportunities with your best employees when you have a short-sighted approach and spend the majority of your time focused on your poor performing employees.

  In my case, I had been added to the high-potential list. In their eyes, that was the justification for being held to a higher standard and being assigned 'extra' tasks.

  While I understand some of the reasons why my division manager did not let me know this sooner, I also felt singled out. I didn't understand at the time that all of the 'extra' assigned tasks were intended to develop my knowledge and skills. This positive could easily have become a negative.

- **RETENTION PROGRAMS THAT DON'T PAYOUT ARE COUNTERPRODUCTIVE (OR NON-CONSEQUENTIAL IN THE BEST CASE SCENARIO).**
  Retention bonuses are usually financial awards given as an incentive to keep employees with the company. They may be cash, stock options, stock grants, or another form of financial compensation. In some cases, retention bonuses are recurring, however most often they are one-time awards.

  Retention bonuses are becoming increasingly popular in business today. This stems from companies wanting to retain key employees who may be tempted to leave during times of uncertainty, difficulty, or change. Retention bonuses may also be paid to key employees with specializations that are critical to ongoing operations.

The stock options I received was a retention bonus intended to keep me employed. I remember being frustrated that they were so far underwater. Obviously, these frustrations were counterproductive with respect to the intent of the award. Ultimately, since the stock options were unlikely to ever pay out, they were of no consequence when I made the decision to leave the company.

Whenever there is an option, I recommend giving retention awards such as cash bonuses or stock grants (*with zero strike price*) that become vested over time.

Bridging the Gap

Performance Appraisal Method: Human-Resources (COST) Accounting Method

The human-resource (COST) accounting method monetizes your employee's performance (*in other words, the value that their employment brings to the company*) and compares it with the cost of retaining the employee.

When your employee's performance is monetized (*evaluated based on cost accounting methods*) factors like unit-wise average service value, quality, overhead cost, interpersonal relationships, and other factors are considered.

Advantages of the human-resources (COST) accounting method are:

- Calculates the cost and value that an employee brings to the company

- Identifies the positive or negative financial impact that an employee's employment has on the company.

There are several disadvantages to the human-resources (COST) accounting method:

- It is easier to quantify the cost of an employee versus the intangible benefits they bring to the company.

- Any future value that the employee may bring to the company may not be included in the current analysis.

"The simple fact is that employees who feel appreciated are more engaged, have lower turnover rates, and generally are more productive."

– Tim Marsh

"I find the harder I
work, the more luck
I seem to have."

– THOMAS JEFFERSON

Chapter 10:

A Hole in the Fence

"Only in an honest and sincere environment, with you providing the example, will people feel comfortable expressing their candid thoughts."

– Tim Marsh

Contemplations:

- *Think of a time in which someone drank too much at a company event. How did the situation get resolved? Were there long-term consequences? If the person was a guest, how did their actions affect the employee?*

- *Have you ever been afraid for your safety while at work? Were you aware of the risk before the incident occurred? How was the situation resolved? Were any changes made as a result?*

The Story...

Location: Venezuela

PERSONAL BACKSTORY: I had never been out of the country when I was asked to go to Venezuela as a training center tutor. Since I had always wanted to travel internationally, I said yes without reservation and failed to ask the most basic questions. In hindsight, my failure to ask questions combined with the management's failure to be forthcoming made for an interesting month.

I was scheduled to fly into Caracas, spend the night, and fly the next day to an airport near El Tigre where the training center and operations base was co-located.

It was a several hour flight from Houston to Caracas. While this was not my first flight, I hadn't flown very often, and I had never flown over water for any significant period of time.

We were still over water when I could feel the plane start to descend. There was no land in sight, but I wasn't panicked. The plane moved lower and lower, yet I still couldn't see any land. I have to admit, I was starting to wonder what was going on.

Looking around, nobody seemed worried, so I went on with reading. The next time I looked out we were getting really low, yet I still couldn't see land. Now, when I looked around, I could see a few others with similar looks on their faces. I kept thinking that if we were in fact going into the water, surely someone would say something.

Just as I was beginning to get really freaked out, the flight attendant finally got on the intercom and told us we were about to land and gave us the usual speech about putting our seat back into the upright position and close our tray tables. Thankfully, I was able to regain my composure in the long taxi to the airport terminal.

While traveling, I was wearing my typical attire which at that time included jeans, a button-up shirt, and a pair of Dr. Martens shoes. I was also carrying my laptop backpack. After retrieving my suitcase, I headed out to find a taxi.

Once inside the taxi, I gave the driver the address of my hotel. He gave me a once over glance and told me that I was mistaken. "No," I said, "this was the name and address I was given for my hotel that night."

> **PERSONAL BACKSTORY:** Unbeknownst to me at the time, somehow our travel agent had booked me into a five-star hotel. Once we arrived, the driver said he would wait as he was certain I had made a mistake. It wasn't a mistake. On both ends of my trip, I stayed at a five-star hotel in a city that was heavily polluted and had entire mountain sides covered in rickety slums (*at night, before I knew what they were, it was a beautiful sight to see all the lights on the mountain sides*). The irony and sense of guilt was not lost on me.

The small plane ride the next day was uneventful. I arrived at a small airport and was met by a driver. We drove until we reached El Tigre, and pulled up to a compound surrounded by eight foot cement block walls with broken glass bottles cemented on the top of the concrete blocks. I noticed that the barbed wire strands on top of the wall were directed inward versus outward as I was accustomed to seeing (*I later was told that when trying to climb back out with loot, this made it more difficult, however I was still skeptical*).

As we got closer, I saw chain link fence gates however there were mattresses, tents, cars, and vans blocking the gate. I was confused and asked the driver what was up. He told me to get out, and we were going to walk from there. We passed through the labyrinth to find a hole in the chain link fence barely large enough for me to climb through.

At this point, I have to be honest that I was really wondering what

I had gotten myself into. After climbing through, I walked to the main office and went inside. Sitting at the front desk was a beautiful young woman. She started to give me the run down and orientation, never mentioning that I had just climbed through a hole in the fence to get in. I remember vividly how she let me know that I shouldn't drink the water, even to brush my teeth, and that when (*not if but when*) I got diarrhea, to come and see her as she had some medicine.

I remember thinking to myself that I there would never come a time that I would walk up and ask her for that medicine. As it turns out, when you forget that mixed drinks have ice made from the local water, you get diarrhea. After several days of having it so bad that you feel like you're going to die, anyone would go to the most beautiful person in the world and ask for the diarrhea medicine.

After she was done with my orientation, she said that Ray, the facility manager, would like to talk with me.

Ray was American. He explained that the local workers were unionized. He went on to say that due to union and government corruption, the local operators were paid the same as the expatriate engineers.

The company had finally taken action to adjust their pay. This resulted in the workers going on strike. At that point, the company declared it to be an illegal strike and fired all the operators. This resulted in the operators barricading the gates. This all transpired about a week before I showed up. In my mind, this was plenty of time for the manager to call and let me know.

Closing **the Gap**

LEADERSHIP TIP 10:

Lead with compassion and empathy, have emotions, and strive for work-life balance for your team.

He didn't. By that time, I had already arrived, so there wasn't much I could do. He told me to have a 'to-go' bag ready, just in case we had to leave the compound in a hurry.

The next morning, I found out that the operating base side of the compound had gotten the wireline trucks out before the gates were barricaded, however they hadn't gotten the downhole tools out. The average open hole wireline tool at that time was slightly larger than three inches in diameter and ranged from about three to twenty feet long. They had thread protectors with hooks on each end. They are used for lifting while connecting the tools together on the rig floor.

Someone had decided that the best way to get the tools out of the compound was to land a helicopter in the compound, chain the tools to the landing gear via the thread protectors, and then have the helicopter ferry them out of the compound. While this worked reasonably well (*there were a few dry runs where they chained too much weight and the helicopter could not lift off*), it served to severely upset the striking operators who thought their actions would prevent the company from being able to catch jobs.

The next morning, the military came to the compound to protect us from striking operators who threatened to storm the compound. Needless to say, eating my bowl of corn flakes next to a soldier with a machine gun was quite surreal.

Fortunately for me, the striking operators didn't have an issue with the training center staff. We were normally free to come and go through the hole in the fence. This gave us the occasional opportunity to go out for food and entertainment.

The food in the compound was horrible. Dinner usually was either chicken or fish (*which unfortunately had the same taste and consistency*) so I really couldn't tell the difference. Once, we were able to schedule a day away at the beach, which allowed us to unwind for a day and get some decent food.

About a week before my stint was over, we had a going away party for one of the instructors. I have never been a heavy drinker, however that night I let the stresses and frustrations of the previous three weeks get the best of me. I started drinking glasses of Johnny Walker. Somewhere around my fourth or fifth glass, I stumbled into Ray and his French wife. With my loosened tongue, I made several true yet not very smart comments. Thankfully for me, they both had so much to drink that they didn't remember what I had said.

Unfortunately, when I called my wife that night from the only phone in the training compound living quarters (*which was located on a counter*), I fell down while telling her I loved her (*in the way someone who has been drinking too much does*). She didn't forget. In fact, we have revisited it periodically over the years since.

...and the Lessons Learned:

- ### CANDOR (AND HONESTY) IS THE BEST POLICY.
  Candor is a personal trait with high-potential for positive impact in your interactions with leaders, colleagues, and subordinates. That said, of all the concepts discussed in this book, candor is presumably the most difficult one that you can be asked to exhibit and implement.

  Why? Likely, it's because candor flies in the face of most of your widely accepted societal norms. Therefore, use of candor will differ because of fear, anxiety, manners, or any number of other excuses.

  Only in an honest and sincere environment, with you providing the example, will people feel comfortable expressing their candid thoughts.

  In my case, had the manager of the training center been candid and honest with me about the strike prior to my departure, I could have made the decision not to go.

In the case that I decided to go, I could have better prepared for the experience.

- **DRINK IN MODERATION (ESPECIALLY AT BUSINESS FUNCTIONS).**
  This was one of the most practical lessons that I have learned in business. Unfortunately, I have also seen many others learn this lesson at the expense of their job, a customer, or another negative result.

  While alcohol is prevalent at many lunches, dinners, and a multitude of other business functions, you must remember that your professional responsibilities have to take precedent over any personal desires thus moderation is always the best option (*this applies even if you are in a position without risk of job loss or repercussions for loss of business, or other reprisals such as being an owner*).

Bridging the Gap
Performance Appraisal Method: 360-Degree Feedback

The 360-degree feedback performance **appraisal** method uses the feedback of approximately 5 to 10 people to evaluate your employee's performance.   In addition, your employee also participates in the appraisal in the form of a self-assessment.

The 360 degree performance appraisal method is an opportunity to understand the employee's strength and weaknesses from multiple vantage points.

The 360-degree feedback performance appraisal methods will vary between companies and industries, however the process to obtain the feedback remains relatively unchanged. The following are the 360-degree feedback process steps:

- **Communication.**
  It's important to communicate the entire 360-degree feedback performance appraisal process (*including the purpose and objective and all the logistics of the process*) to all of the stakeholders involved.

- **Feedback Personnel Selection.**
  The selection of the reviewers is a critical part of the 360-degree feedback performance appraisal process. The minimum number of reviewers will include the employee and at least one subordinate, colleague, and supervisor. The actual number of reviewers will depend on a number of factors.

- **Material Distribution.**
  The distribution of materials will vary between different companies (*and may even vary within individual companies*). The options range from hard copy questionnaires to fully online systems.

- **Completion of Questionnaire.**
  Once the survey has been sent to the reviewers, it's then their responsibility to complete and submit the questionnaire. This part of the process usually takes the longest to complete; therefore, it's recommended to establish a completion deadline for this process. If the materials and directive to complete the questionnaire is from a senior executive, it usually helps with ensuring this step is completed expeditiously.

- **ANALYSIS AND REPORT GENERATION.**

Once the individual questionnaires have been completed and collated, a confidential, composite report should be generated. In addition, the data should be analyzed for consistent and anomaly trends. The trend data should be consolidated into a separate report for the employee's manager.

- **COMMUNICATION OF RESULTS.**

The summary report should be given to the employee during an in-person private meeting with the employee's supervisor and a representative from human resources. During the meeting, the report results should be freely discussed. All trends should be discussed and a development plan generated. Anomaly trends should be discussed with the intent of understanding the causes for the opposing vantage points. If applicable, additional development plan action items should be generated. Anomaly trends that are not able to be resolved should be noted for review again during the next re-evaluation.

- **DEVELOPMENT PLAN.**

During the communication of results process, development plan action items should be agreed upon and documented. They should be concise, time based, with personnel assignments and deadlines. The plan is co-owned by the employee, their manager, and human resources with each having an important role. The employee is responsible for taking the lead in completing the action items. The employee's manager must provide the necessary leadership and resources to enable the employee to complete the plan. Human resources should monitor the status of the plan action items and work to support the employee and manager.

- **FOLLOW-UP EVALUATION.**

  The 360-degree feedback system is not a one-time event. It is important that the process continues periodically to measure progress made with the development plans. In addition, unresolved anomaly trends should be re-evaluated during subsequent 360-degree feedback evaluations to monitor whether the trends have converged, remained the same, or diverged further. Anomaly trends that appear in multiple 360-degree feedback performance appraisals should be further investigated to obtain resolution to the root cause(s).

There are numerous advantages to a 360-degree assessment:

- Provides a comprehensive view of employee performance.

- It improves the credibility of the performance appraisal system by incorporating input from multiple sources.

- Colleague, subordinate, and self-assessment aids with overall employee development.

- Variety of vantage points can be gathered from different reviewers.

- Here not only managers but colleagues are also responsible for assessment of staff performance, which empowers them.

- Gives a voice to employees from whom may not typically be heard.

- Creates a culture of candor

Disadvantages of 360-degree assessment:

- Complex and time intensive appraisal method

- Lack of process confidentiality concerns leads to hesitancy with providing honest feedback.

- A lot of effort is required in order to train employees to effectively use the 360 degree appraisal system.

- Multi-step process requires large commitment of support services time and resources.

"When establishing your company's brand, the distinction between knowing and understanding how your products and services are used by your customers is paramount."

– Tim Marsh

Chapter 11:

Taking Advantage of Employees

"Employees that are continually frustrated may not have any outward signs, such as loss of productivity or poor attitude."

– TIM MARSH

Contemplations:

- *Have you ever had your loyalty taken advantage of by a leader? Do you know the reason? What was the outcome? How did it affect your job results, performance, and satisfaction?*

- *Recall a time in which you were made a promise by a leader that wasn't kept. What was the promise? Why wasn't it kept? Were there any long-term consequences?*

RALPH IS SILENTLY SCREAMING
WITH HIS MARKER EVERY DAY.

The Story...

Location: Various

For better or worse, I've been on both sides of the "taking advantage of an employee" coin. Based on this experience, I think it's human nature for leaders to migrate towards comfort, ease, and leverage (*leverage being more of a manipulative trait used to artificially create the equivalent of a loyal employee*).

These are the primary reasons many leaders take advantage of their loyal employees. The challenge arises when the leader or employee is not self-aware of the situation.

I can honestly say that I feel that my loyalty (*in some way or another*) has been taken advantage of by leaders at every company I've worked for since I was sixteen. Don't get me wrong, I don't mean to sound like a victim. In fact, quite was the opposite.

I was sufficiently self-aware to understand what was happening. As was the case with me, being a loyal employee can benefit your career. It did with mine.

PERSONAL BACKSTORY: As a junior field engineer (JFE), I was informed that I didn't get days off until I broke out as a field engineer (FE) (*this was an unofficial rule that wasn't disclosed until arrival at the district*). This was a far cry from the standard 9 and 3 schedule the recruiters and I had discussed during the interview process.

As I came to understand, this hazing process had been going on forever. In many ways not having days off was not that bad compared to the various unpleasant job tasks I was given. It was like everyone thought they were my supervisor.

Example 1 – As a new employee, eager to make a good impression, I worked hard and tried to do everything I was asked to do. I had grown up in a strict household where you did what you were told so that easily carried over into the workplace. A fundamental difference between the two was that at home, my parents did not take advantage of this, however at work, it was a different story.

Everyone had some menial task they didn't want to do that they assigned me as part of my "training". As I would observe later, the hazing that I endured was not an isolated event nor as bad as it could have been. Other loyal, hardworking JFEs fell into the same trap I did. Occasionally, I did see some stand up and resist the system.

While I'm not proud of my actions (*and to help resolve my guilty feelings, I don't think I gave as bad as I got*), I perpetuated the practice while I worked in the field.

The JFEs that would do whatever they were asked (*whether from leverage or out of sense of loyalty or duty*), and I got all the jobs that I didn't like or want to do. These "training" tasks ranged from typing mondain company and well information into the computer, to getting the mud data from the rig floor, to sampling the mud, to even running to grab us drinks.

JFEs that resisted, while still having to do some, didn't spend near as much time on these sort of tasks. In the long run though, these JFEs didn't get away from bucking the system unscathed.

Closing the Gap

LEADERSHIP TIP 11:

Be a mentor, don't hesitate to get your hands dirty, and develop your team and yourself.

Example 2 – Rafe is a colleague that I worked with for a number of years. At the time, he was a forty-five year old bachelor that was married to his work. He routinely spent twelve hour days at the office and had an encyclopedic knowledge. Prior to his time at our company, Rafe had spent twenty plus years in a similar position at a competitor. He had been caught up in a restructuring and downsizing layoff.

His hiring manager at our company was long gone when I met Rafe, however his actions were still having an impact. At the time he was laid off, the industry was in a slow period. This combined with Rafe's very specialized area of expertise meant there were not many employment opportunities available outside of the one at our company.

With this knowledge, the hiring manager took advantage of the situation (*Rafe needed a job*) by offering him a salary that was significantly less than he was making previously. Not only this, but his salary was significantly less than what was comparable for others in the industry with his experience and expertise. To complicate matters even further, his offer was less than what others in the company were earning.

Years later, when we first met, Rafe was still struggling to get his salary back to where it was when he was laid off. Although he was very loyal (*which is why he stayed*), he also knew that he had been taken advantage of by the hiring manager.

Example 3 – Jason was one of my subordinates and also a close personal friend. When I accepted my position, I knew I had taken a risk. Very quickly after starting, I realized that I had made a big mistake. At that point, I had two choices. I knew I had the knowledge and ability to fix it, so that was option one. Option two was to abandon ship. Ultimately I chose to stay. With this decision, I knew I would need to hire quality people I could rely on.

Jason and I had previously worked together at another company before I hired him. He was doing well in the position I hired him for, however I eventually convinced him to take on the role of safety manager for the company (*I needed someone who not only was competent but that I could trust in this position*). I felt it was a perfect position for him. Jason had tons of technical knowledge. He truly cared about the safety of employees, and had the guts to work through the immense challenges we were facing.

From a safety standpoint (*and in hindsight every other standpoint*), the company was a mess. Although I had driven lots of progress from the operations side, the culture was still fragmented.

The owners' first priority was to make money, their second priority was to make money, and their third priority was?

You guessed it, to make money. Any commitment to anything else was purely lip service to the employees, our customers, and likely to themselves.

The district managers who made the most money for the company (*regardless of the risk to their employees or company*) were put on a pedestal. Support functions were second class employees. The safety department was there only in case of an emergency (*which to them was anything that got in the way of making money*).

I used to think the safety department was like one of the 'break glass in case of emergency' boxes. When operations got in a bind from their free-wheeling antics, the owners wanted to be able to break the glass, release the safety department to come pick up the pieces and fix or smooth over any issues with the government acronym types.

Once done, they wanted to be able to put them back in the box and install a new pane of glass. Essentially, the safety department was to be seen but not heard unless in case of emergency.

I knew that the owners would change their stance on safety and compliance (*because it would eventually cost them money*) but in the meantime, it was my job to improve our operations and stay in compliance enough to keep our explosive permit and DOT operating authority.

This meant that he (*and his department, albeit on a lessor scale*) and I would be spread thin for a while. In those days, our explosive operations were constantly being audited by the ATF and our trucks inspected by the DOT. In general, we were not having major compliance violations. Paperwork errors was always an issue with explosives. Simple violations (*that would have been caught even with a cursory pre-trip*) was an issue with our trucks.

For a long while, it seemed as though Jason and I were driving all over the country day and night trying to stay ahead of the next audit.

I remember a time we were both outside of Houston working on explosive paperwork and inventory counts in one of our districts. It was about 5pm when I got the call from our northwestern Oklahoma district manager. He said the ATF was going to be there in the morning to audit his operations. I could tell that he was worried. We looked at each other to decide who was going.

PERSONAL BACKSTORY: **Even though I was the leader, I've always found that operating as a team gets better results. Therefore, in this situation, I wasn't going to pull rank to avoid driving all night to Oklahoma.**

Jason lost the coin toss or whatever we used to decide. I remember telling him it was only an eight-hour drive. Of course, we had both been up all day and when he got there at 3 am, he still would have to do an internal audit of the counts and paperwork and fix any issues. We never stopped at the time to consider the existential dilemma of the safety and operational leadership performing unsafe acts in an effort to keep the company in compliance.

I remember I used to tell Jason that I was stretching him (*this was a reference to the stretch objectives we used to always achieve at our previous employer*). He would quip that eventually even rubber bands break when stretched too far.

Was I taking advantage of his loyalty and friendship?

Definitely…!

How could I get by with it?

He knew I was working just as hard as he was, and he too believed what we were doing was critical for the employees and company (*it also helped that we were friends*). At times, we literally felt like we were keeping the company from self-destructing with our efforts.

Eventually, the owners did come around to the need for safety and safe operations. The irony is that once they did, they wanted immediate results in a business that had been operating 180 degrees from where they should have been since inception.

It was not long afterwards that Jason and I both left the company. In the intervening time, the industry slowed down, and it appears the owners have reverted back to their old ways.

Only time will tell their long-term fate.

…and the Lessons Learned:

- **Nobody wants to be frustrated every day.**
  While this may be a simple concept, you would be surprised how few leaders actively seek feedback from their employees regarding topics such as frustrations, feeling appreciated, etc.

  Employees that are continually frustrated may not have any outward signs, such as loss of productivity or poor attitude. Depending on their work ethic and personality, they may suffer in silence. One thing is certain, very few people, whether it's visible or not, will work indefinitely for a company in which they are frustrated on a regular basis. Eventually the loyalty, friendship, money, or other factors keeping the employee will be overcome.

Remember, in order for you to see the maximum potential of your people, you need to have your finger on the pulse of their feelings. Knowing them, their families, their hopes and dreams should be the norm not the exception.

Seriously, if you don't want to know more about your people and want to take better care of them, either you have the wrong people on your team or your company has the wrong leader.

- **STRETCH EMPLOYEES WITHOUT BREAKING THEM.**
Stretching your employees is fine as long as you stay within their elastic limit. They can do the task or assignments, and while maybe outside their comfort zone, once done they are back to normal. This is where you should strive to always be.

Straining your employees is different. In this case, you have permanently changed them. This can take many different appearances, but here are a few examples.

Take one of your employees that is continually frustrated. One day, they are done with you (*or the company*) and start looking for another job. They come to you and resign. This time you are able to convince them to stay. Even though they stay, will they ever be the same employee? *No...!*

What about the employee who gets injured on the job? They may make a full recovery and return to work, but are they ever going to be the same? What if the injury cost them an eye or a leg? Are they ever going to be the same at work? What about their home life, is it ever going to be the same? No, never...!

These are just a couple examples of pushing your people too far and as a result, they are forever changed. Remember, sometimes they are forever changed outside of work as well.

Lastly, is when employees are broken. This is when the ten-year employee is crying in your office. It's when the high-potential employee that you have never differentiated gets that headhunter call and feels like someone finally sees their value and efforts as they type their resignation letter. It's when you knock on a door to tell a spouse their loved one isn't coming home.

In my career, I have seen, done, or been the person in each of these examples.

The time to act is now, the time to change is now, the time to be better is now, as there is no guarantee to be able to do so tomorrow.

Bridging the Gap
Leadership Styles

Leadership impacts all aspects of business, including closing your business gaps.

In addition to conveying my leadership lessons learned, I want to discuss the ten leadership styles (*or types*) shown in Figure 2:

Figure 2

Each styles has their own unique characteristics. These characteristics influence the leader's actions. As such, it is critical that you understand each since they are fundamental leadership concepts.

"Companies must actively seek and identify great leaders; then have the insight and courage to allow them to lead."

– Tim Marsh

"The best way to predict the future is to create it."

– PETER DRUCKER

Chapter 12:

Individual vs Team Contributions

"Often when a leader delays making a tough decision, the primary reason is solely for their own benefit."

– Tim Marsh

Contemplations:

- *Consider a time in which you were misunderstood due to someone making an assumption. How did it make you feel? What was the outcome?*

- *Recall a time in which you made an impulse comment or decision. Do you struggle with impulse control? How did this situation turn out? In hindsight, do you wish you had taken more time before you spoke or acted?*

Mind the Gap

"I'M SORRY, SIR, I CAN'T INSPECT YOUR WATER LINES.
I JUST READ THE METER."

The Story...
Location: Canada

A number of years ago, I was working as the northeast division engineer based out of the Charleston, West Virginia district and also supporting our Bradford, Pennsylvania operation.

PERSONAL BACKSTORY: My manager at the time, Bob, was a chain-smoking womanizer from NYC whose favorite saying was "ya, ya, ya...". Like many of the employees of the Charleston district, he didn't live locally. This was a result of several district closures in Ohio, Michigan, and even West Virginia. After the closures, many of the longtime employees from those districts worked remotely until they could retire.

Bob was having an affair with Valerie, one of our female employees. With his family living out of state (*he went home to Ohio on the weekends*) and his extracurricular activities, Bob was not at the district as much as he should have been (*I'm not sure where he spent his time or even where he lived when in Charleston as he wouldn't tell anyone*).

Whenever he wasn't at the district, he often didn't answer his phone. Many of us used to joke that we should call Valerie and ask her to pass him the phone.

One night, there was a vehicle accident, and I was trying to reach him. As expected, he didn't answer his phone. I remember trying to figure out how to tactfully handle calling Valerie in order to get a hold of him. Finally, I called her and told her what was going on. I told her that if she heard from Bob to have him call me right away. He called about a minute after we hung up.

I usually ran the day-to-day operations, despite it being Bob's responsibility. Thus, when the division human resources manager scheduled a visit, it was mostly left up to me to make sure everything was in order and prepared for her visit.

Her visit went well, and before she left we had a half hour or so to sit down and discuss my career and how things were going. My current position had been my first promotion outside of field operations. I'm not sure why (*as I hadn't ever been there*) but as she was leaving, I casually mentioned to her that I wouldn't mind working in Canada someday.

The following week, I was working in our Pennsylvania location when my manager called. He asked me to stand by the fax machine. As the paper printed out, I really could not imagine what he would be faxing me. As it turns out, it was my promotion to location manager and transfer letter. In Canada...!

Closing ▶ the Gap

LEADERSHIP TIP 12:

Avoid company politics, have the courage to stand by your principles, and accept responsibility.

Oh no, my wife is going to kill me, I thought. When I looked up where Wainwright, Alberta was located (*population approximately 5200 people and located in the middle of nowhere*), I was even more convinced I was a dead man. As it turns out, my plight was going to get worse before it got better.

The only house available for rent in town was right next to one of the busiest east-west railroad lines in Alberta. To make matters worse, that summer had temperatures near 100 degrees for three straight weeks. Let me just say that my wife loves to be cool (*my parents had asked for extra blankets whenever they visited once in the summertime*). The first time it started getting warm in the house, she flipped the thermostat to cool to turn on the air. Nothing but fan.

She immediately was on the phone with the landlord to discuss the problem.

As she got a faint look on her face, I knew something was wrong. When she hung up, I asked her what was wrong. She told me that when she asked the landlord to fix the air conditioner he asked, "What air conditioner?". Evidently, the cool on the thermostat didn't do anything but turn on the fan. As it turns out, many homes in Canada only have heat and no air conditioning.

It was a long summer. Fortunately for me, there was plenty of work to keep me occupied at the office.

While it was taking a while to adjust to living in Canada, I enjoyed both the people I worked with and the work itself. I like to take time to understand before I demand to be understood. As a result, I spent much of my early days getting to know people. One operator that I got to hear about from virtually everyone was Lew, a French-Canadian guy. He seemed to be on everyone's bad side. I had heard numerous tales of his temper and bad deeds. Despite the tales of his negative behavior, almost everyone did mention that he was very competent. As I would learn, most of the good and bad I heard about him was spot on.

Leading people is one of the most challenging components of being in management. This is especially true when one of your people is very talented yet very flawed.

I tried for months to mentor and coach Lew. To his credit, he tried. When he worked alone, he was stellar. When he worked with others, his work was also stellar, but his behavior brought down everyone else on the team. Eventually, despite his individual performance and all my efforts, I had to let Lew go. We were a team-oriented business. I simply did not have enough individual work to offset his negative effect on the entire team. It was a very difficult decision that I struggled with for some time before implementing.

...and the Lessons Learned:

- **LEADERS SHOULD UNDERSTAND BEFORE DEMANDING TO BE UNDERSTOOD.**
As most leaders will admit, they have learned from other's mistakes, but not nearly as much as from their own failures and mistakes.

  One of the biggest mistakes I made in my early leadership efforts was to demand to be understood by my team before I understood the dynamics of the team or operation I was supposed to be leading.

  Like many leaders, I thought I was put in place because I had all the answers. I didn't need to take time to get to know anything, I already knew everything.

  Fortunately for me, I have had the privilege of working for some outstanding teams who were used to know-it-all leaders. In general, they have been gracious enough not to let me fall on my own sword.

  I am also fortunate that they were savvy enough to let me know they kept me out of a bind (*so I could learn my lesson, which hopefully I have...*) while allowing me to save face with others outside the team and up the chain of command. For this, I am lucky and grateful.

- **DON'T DELAY MAKING TOUGH DECISIONS.**
Often when a leader delays making a tough decision, the primary reason is solely for their own benefit. These delays are harmful for both the leader and their team.

This is exactly what happened in my case when I delayed making the decision to terminate Lew. The delay was solely for my benefit. And yes, the delay was harmful for both me and the team.

The team suffered by having to continue working with the employee's poor behavior. This lowered morale and productivity as a result.

The decision delay hindered my ability to effectively lead the team (*at least for a period of time*) as I came off as apprehensive and indecisive. These are definitely not the characteristics of a great leader.

Bridging the Gap
Leadership Style: Laissez–Faire

The laissez-faire leadership style may also be known as the delegative leadership style. It is characterized by leaders who demonstrate a hands-off approach and allow their employees to make many of their own decisions.

The laissez-faire leadership style relies on leaders having confidence in their team to possess and utilize the skills, knowledge, creativity, and motivation necessary to complete assignments without significant oversight from the leader.

The advantages of the laissez-faire leadership style are:

- **GROWTH, INNOVATION, AND DEVELOPMENT.**
  Due to the leader's hands-off approach, employees are encouraged (*or may feel forced*) to not only use, but also to grow and develop their skill sets. Without significant ongoing guidance from the leader, employees are encouraged (*or again may feel forced*) to innovate and use creative solutions (*from themselves and others*) to solve problems.

- **AUTONOMY AND AUTHORITY.**
  Employees have the autonomy and authority to make their own decisions, which speeds up the decision process.

Disadvantages of the laissez-faire leadership style are:

- **UNCERTAINTY AND COHESIVENESS.**
  A significant issue with the laissez-faire leadership style is team members often feel uncertain about the decisions they've made or even their roles and responsibilities within the team. This is further complicated by the lack of cohesiveness often found with laissez-faire leaders and their team. Uncertainty rarely increases team cohesiveness.

- **RESPONSIBILITY, MOTIVATION, AND PERFORMANCE.**
  Employees who report to a laissez-faire leader may lack motivation and productivity. This can be perpetuated since the leader may resist accepting responsibility for team mistakes. A laissez-faire leader may cause inefficiency if they don't define the work scope so that it is understood by all team members.

The laissez-faire leadership style works best when leaders provide the necessary upfront knowledge and resources to a team that is motivated, knowledgeable, highly skilled, and creative. In contrast, the laissez-faire leadership style doesn't work well in situations where their team requires regular leader oversight and involvement.

"When employees embrace the attitudes and behaviors derived from the company's core values, leadership has effectively safeguarded the company from migrating away from them over time."

– TIM MARSH

Mind the Gap:
Leadership Basics II

Golden Rule Leaders

Golden rule leaders incorporate the best traits of each leadership style. In addition (*and this is the essential differentiator*), they incorporate the biblical golden rule into their actions and decisions.

[12]Therefore all things whatsoever ye would that men should do to you, do ye even so to them: for this is the law and the prophets. [13]Enter ye in at the strait gate: for wide is the gate, and broad is the way, that leadeth to destruction, and many there be which go in thereat: [14]Because strait is the gate, and narrow is the way, which leadeth unto life, and few there be that find it.

MATTHEW 7:12-14, KING JAMES VERSION (KJV)

By integrating the leadership traits with the wisdom of these verses into their actions and decisions, these leaders are able to maximize their employees' results while minimizing personnel business gaps.

Golden rule leaders focus on the needs of all their leadership stakeholders (*these include shareholders, employees, company leaders, customers, vendors, and the general public*).

It's important to understand that these leaders aren't weak nor timid nor do they avoid tough or unpopular decisions. Instead, they take decisive action, make righteous decisions, and give candid feedback.

Celebrate Your Victories

Business is tough…!

With frequent shifts in the economy, increasingly tougher competition, changes in society, pandemics, and other new hurdles coming more frequently, you have to celebrate your victories.

These celebrations should include all employees involved with the victory (*and when possible, family members*). They can range from mild, small gatherings at work to an elaborate celebration party at a nice offsite venue. Regardless of how you choose to celebrate, they allow your employees an opportunity to blow off steam while giving you the opportunity to show appreciation (*including rewards and recognition*).

Leading with Transparency

Employee trust and your credibility can be diminished by a lack of transparency.

Here are seven ways you can improve transparency:

- Insist on honest and integrity
- Empower your employees to make decisions
- Provide detailed results (*even if they are not good*)
- Establish effective communication at all levels
- Eliminate organizational silos
- Understand appropriate privacy requirements
- Provide access to company information

Internal Branding

Your brand will convey valuable information to potential applicants about your company.

This information will filter many potential applicants that do not share your company values and beliefs. In addition, this applicant filtering improves the efficiency of the interview and hiring processes. Lastly, it provides for more informed new hire employees.

If you have new hire candidates that already know and share the company's values, the likelihood for their retention increases significantly.

As new hire employees progress with the company, their level of trust and loyalty will increase when the company exhibits the values and beliefs conveyed by your brand. This trust and loyalty culminates into higher employee job satisfaction and productivity.

Avoiding Miscommunication

These are common causes of workplace miscommunication:

- Failing to explain expectations fully
- Making assumptions
- Failure to use the most efficient communication method
- Trying to speak in too technical of vernacular
- Use of non-verbal communication (*gestures*)
- Being too timid to speak candidly
- Reluctance due to adversarial relationship between employees and leadership
- Information sent to wrong person
- Too large of a distribution to be effective

Work-Life Balance

There is a direct connection between workplace flexibility perks and work-life balance. Work-life balance describes the challenge between spending time with life activities such as family, friends, church, sports, and other outside-of-work activities and work related tasks.

Work-life balance and workplace flexibility perks vary greatly based on job industry, location, and position however virtually every job has potential to have them in some form.

Keep in mind, no matter how much the company cares, nobody cares more about your work-life balance and flexibility perks than you do.

Non-Financial Benefits

Non-financial benefits (*commonly referred to as perks*) are alternative methods to compensate your employees beyond their financial compensation (*paychecks, bonuses, commissions, etc.*) and benefits. Two primary objectives for providing perks are to attract diverse candidates and retain high-quality employees.

Perks that are especially effective for retaining your high-quality employees are *'workplace flexibility'* perks. These include working from home, additional vacation days, flex-time, alternate work hours, etc.

Job Security and Stability

Job security is the likelihood that you will stay employed. Job stability is the assurance that you have in your maintaining preferred job or occupation. They consistently rank as high importance in employee satisfaction surveys. There are numerous conditions and factors that can influence your job security. Several examples of these are:

- Economic conditions
- Awarded work and contracts
- Collective bargaining agreement (union)
- Public or private sector

Job security will continue to decrease over time due to changes in business practices combined with employee priority changes.

While you may not be able to provide job security to all employees, your retention efforts (*such as retention bonuses, employment contracts, etc.*) should focus on your high-quality, key employees.

Groupthink and Consensus Decisions

Groupthink often occurs due to a misguided *(and often unintentional)* priority of the leaders to choose team cohesiveness and unanimity over making the best decision.

An important take away is that leaders must not confuse allowing team members freely express and debate various ideas, thoughts, and viewpoints with the requirement that all team members concur with the decision made by the group.

In many cases, the best decision will not be a consensus decision.

"You will either step forward into growth or you will step back into safety."

– ABRAHAM MASLOW

Chapter 13:

An Alternative Path

"Improving or eliminating your negative attributes will not only make you a better leader, but also a better person."

– Tim Marsh

Contemplations:

- *Recall a time in which you misjudged someone. How did you realize your mistake? What did you do once you found out? What lasting impact did your misjudgment have?*

- *Consider a mistake that you have made in which you have taken time to self-reflect. What was the cause? Have you made the same or a similar mistake since? How often do you use self-reflection?*

Mind the Gap

SOMETIMES THE BEST PATH DEPENDS
ON WHETHER YOU HAVE 4-WHEEL-DRIVE.

The Story...
Location: Various

Many leaders (*myself included*) struggle with giving their employees the flexibility to achieve the desired results via alternative paths. These leaders tell their employees what to do and how to do it in order to get tasks completed. Over time, this can translate to leaders thinking their way is the only correct way.

In some companies, these struggles permeate from the top. In these cases, the mid-level leaders are told what to do and how to do it by their manager. They in turn perpetuates this behavior throughout the entire company.

While there have been multiple times in my career I have been guilty of this, it occurred more often than not with people who perform tasks that I am not comfortable or competent with personally (*in my case it is most often with salespeople*).

When I moved to Canada to start my first location manager role, I was eager to perform well. I met my field salesman on the first day of the new job. He had about thirty years of seniority, with all but the last few years in the field. He was a quirky, outdoorsy man that was very laid back. He liked to say he was "finer than a frog's hair". On that first day, he didn't have his dog with him at the office, but I met Rufus soon afterwards.

Being the uptight, insufferable manager I was, this really bothered me. The concept of bringing your pet to work with you every day was new to me. Due to his seniority, the power dynamics in the district was that everyone liked and respected him.

I decided that his dog wasn't the battle to fight this early in my tenure, so I grudgingly let it go. Besides Rufus, there was another one of his quirks that drove me crazy. His work hours, which in total quantity were fine, normally consisted of arriving around 10 am and leaving at 6 or 7 pm. Again, the uptight, insufferable manager portion of me wanted to tell him we started work at 8 am.

I just couldn't get past these unusual behaviors. One day after about three months I had seen enough, I was going to bring him in and give him a warning letter. I sat down and started filling out the progressive disciplinary form. As I was answering the questions, it dawned on me that outside of these quirks, his performance and results were superb.

Closing the Gap

LEADERSHIP TIP 13:

The little things matter, check-in often, empower your people, and explain the 'why'.

As I put the form in my drawer, I started to think about the situation. I self-reflected on why his quirks bothered me so badly. Then I started to understand that it was only me that his behavior bothered. At this point, I started wonder whether I was as much a part of the problem as he was.

Needless to say, it didn't take much self-reflection to realize my actions did not represent what was best for the company insomuch as what was best for me. Now who wasn't doing their job...?

Later in my career, I would run across another situation involving a young salesperson who was quirky. While I would like to say that I learned the lesson from my Canadian days, I hadn't.

This salesman was everything I wasn't.

- *I was technically strong; he focused on the basics.*
- *I was at the office every day; he worked from home.*
- *I wore work clothes and boots; he wore shorts and flip-flops.*
- *I liked meetings and reports; he preferred phone calls.*
- *I have black and white ethics; he lives in a gray world.*
- *I am a business conservative; he likes to wheel and deal.*

The list could go on and on. It's safe to say that his differences frustrated me and others in the past. The challenge from my standpoint is that, like my other salesman, his results were good.

Did he have his challenges?

Yes, of course.

Was I overly sensitive to any of his mistakes?

Yes, however, it was my problem, not his...!

Like before, the obvious question that should always be asked is whether your actions and objections are what's best for the company or what's best for you? As for me, if I am not careful, I can easily be guilty of doing what's best for me.

...and the Lessons Learned:

- **LEADERS SHOULD CONSTANTLY BE EVALUATING THEIR MOTIVES.**
  There are lessons that most leaders learn very quickly. One such lesson is that just because you're a leader, it doesn't mean that you don't make mistakes.

  While some lessons are obvious, others can elude leaders for all of their career. These elusive lessons require honest self-reflection that evaluates your motivations, biases, priorities, prejudices, and intentions.

  Once you have completed your self-reflection evaluation, you focus on your positive attributes and address your negative ones. Be forewarned, though, you will also identify things about yourself during this process that you don't want to know. Rest assured that we all have them, and only by knowing them can you work to improve or eliminate them.

There is an upside to all of this effort. Improving or eliminating your negative attributes will not only make you a better leader, but also a better person.

- ### Just because it is different, doesn't mean it's wrong.

A lesson more applicable in business today than ever is the need to be willing to accept things that are different than what may be traditional.

Change and acceptance of differences is nothing new in business. Look at the different ways companies operated due to the pandemic. Who would have guessed that large numbers of office workers throughout major cities would be working from home? How many companies resisted work from home for whatever reason? Many, when forced to have their employees work from home, saw it as a better option. In the end, we learned that many companies had been resistant to working from home because it was different than what was done historically. They thought because it was different, it was wrong.

Other business areas, such as dress expectations, have also seen tremendous change. Look at the differences in dress today versus in the past (*three-piece suits have changed to business casual or casual*). Even between industries today there are big differences. Think of how different the dress expectations are at many high-tech companies. In some of these companies, employees routinely wear shorts and flip-flops to work.

Despite the changes we have seen, I still see people who think, dress, talk, or act differently denied equal opportunity because of those differences.

Bridging the Gap
Leadership Style: Autocratic

The autocratic leadership style may also be known as the authoritarian leadership style. It is characterized by leaders that desire to make all decisions (*usually they prefer little to no input when making decisions*).

The advantages of the autocratic leadership style are:

- **REGIMENTED STRUCTURE.**
  Leaders with an autocratic leadership style usually create a highly structured, rigid work environment. In this environment, they set and communicate well define boundaries and expectations. Autocratic leaders work well in industries with tasks or projects that have set deadlines, rules, and/or specifications.

- **RELIEVES DECISION MAKING BURDEN.**
  The autocratic leadership style works well in high intensity environments, where people benefit from being relieved of the burden of having to make numerous decisions. By having a leader making the majority of the decisions, employees are able to focus on performing their job duties. These environments are usually high stress such as military combat units, fire fighter and ambulance personnel, hospital emergency rooms, and police SWAT teams.

- **PROVIDES GUIDANCE.**
  An autocratic leadership style is effective in small groups (*such as at a school, church, or organization*) where a leadership hierarchy is not formally established. In these type of groups, failure to have a leader can result in a lack of results. In this situation, the autocratic leader can take on the task of appointing roles and responsibilities, assigning tasks, and establishing timelines.

Disadvantages of the autocratic leadership style are:

- **LACKS DECISION DIVERSITY.**
  The autocratic leadership style lacks decision diversity, as the leader typically makes all of the decisions. This lack of input results in a lack of creativity. This lack of creativity is likely a source of frustration to employees who may have more creative alternative suggestions. Another disadvantage of autocratic leaders not soliciting input is they may overlook skills and expertise of their employees.

- **DIFFICULT ON EMPLOYEES.**
  Competent employees working for an autocratic leader can become easily frustrated since they are not allowed to fully contribute. Employees reporting to an autocratic leader may also feel they are not trusted or respected because of the lack of autonomy and input. These feelings of frustration, the lack of trust, and lack of respect can lead to poor employee morale and performance. They can also result in high turnover of the most competent and talented employees.

"Customer loyalty is the flywheel for your sales efforts."

– TIM MARSH

Chapter 14:

The 3 F's

"By being out front of the problem, you can either accept responsibility and immediately work to resolve the problem or mount a vigorous defense of your innocence early in the process."

– Tim Marsh

Contemplations:

- *Think of a positive experience you have had with a salesperson. What techniques did they use that were the most effective? How likely are you to buy from them again? Was the product they were selling equal to or better than their competition?*

- *Have you witnessed inappropriate sales tactics? What about it was inappropriate? Did their tactics produce better results? How did their sales tactics make you feel?*

Mind the Gap

LEE ROY IS ABOUT TO FAIL
THE SALES TRAINING COURSE

The Story...

Location: Pennsylvania

PERSONAL BACKSTORY: I often tell strangers that I wouldn't be a good salesman because I don't like people. While not true (*most of the time*), the comments are normally off-putting enough to change the subject. The truth of the matter is that I enjoy the fundamentals and management of sales. I don't like the random small talk, rejection, kissing up, and taking one for the team.

During my time as the northeast area manager, I was responsible for all aspects of the business, including sales.

The sales manager, Clark, was a member of the family that had sold their business to our company. He had held the same position for many years before the acquisition. As a result, he was very well connected throughout the region and our product line enjoyed a dominant market position.

Closing the Gap

LEADERSHIP TIP 14:

Good leaders develop good leaders. Give 100% and do the job you are capable of rather than just what is expected.

All of his field salesmen had transitioned into equivalent positions with the new company. Most were long-term operational field employees that migrated into sales as a less physical transitional role to their retirement. As a result, the sales approach and effectiveness of each varied tremendously. Since most of the open hole work in the area was awarded via annual contracts, the field sales roles were less critical for day to day jobs and focused more on account maintenance and cased hole work.

One of the corporate initiatives was for operations management and sales personnel to attend a sales training seminar. For the seminar taught in the northeast, I signed up along with Clark and his entire team. We were joined at the seminar by personnel from other northeast product lines.

Based on the dynamics of my sales organization, their backgrounds and seniority, I didn't have high expectations for the sales training seminar. It turned out to be very memorable.

The primary theme of the training was "position your competition before they position you". While the concept itself was not mind-blowing, the way they chose to present it was provocative. Other less memorable themes focused on adaptive sales techniques and concentrating on product and service strengths.

At one point during the seminar, we were asked to split up into two-person groups. Part of the exercise was to conduct a survey of your partner. The survey included get-to-know-you questions about their family and background, as well as questions about their selling technique.

My partner was Rick, one of my field salesmen who consistently had the highest sales numbers. He was from one of our districts that offered multiple services. We both took a few minutes to complete the survey, then exchanged them to go over the results.

As I read through his questionnaire, I noticed that when asked to describe his sales technique, he had written down "I use the 3 Fs".

My obvious question was to ask what the 3 Fs were. Rick started off by saying that in his experience, virtually any customer will want to talk about one of the 3 Fs. He continued on by saying that he would talk about one of the 3 Fs then ask for work. That's it he said, my entire sales technique.

The first 'F' was fishing.

Rick said that he loved to fish. Whenever he was with customers who liked to fish, they discussed fishing during sales calls.

The second 'F' was fighting.

Rick enjoyed boxing. If fishing was off the table, many customers liked to talk about fighting (*boxing, domestic disputes, etc.*).

The third 'F' is fornicating. [This is the censored version.]

Rick said that if all else fails, almost any company man would talk about women.

> **AN IMPORTANT PERSONAL NOTE:** Let me be clear. I have always spoken out against and prohibited the exploitation of women in general and specifically for sales or business advancement. This includes, but is not limited to, hiring women specifically to exploit their sexuality, soliciting prostitution, or visiting strip clubs.

...and the Lessons Learned:

- **TAKE PROACTIVE ACTION TO POSITION YOURSELF BEFORE YOU ARE POSITIONED.**
Over the course of my career, I have found that being proactive has given me the ability to make decisions and take actions versus sitting back and having them made for me by my competition, customers, or others.

  One of the best applications of being proactive is when you experience problems or crisis situations. I have always felt that "running to your problems" has served me better than delaying or running away from them. In this manner, you can head off many of the difficulties before they are out of your control. By being out front of the problem, you can either accept responsibility and immediately work to resolve the problem, or mount a vigorous defense of your innocence early in the process. The optics associated with this type of proactive response will gain you goodwill in most instances.

  To demonstrate this point, consider how you feel when you hear news reports such as "Company X self-reported the violation and is actively cooperating with the agency to rectify the problem." This type of response usually gives the impression that the company is accepting responsibility.

If the decision were up to you, would the consequences be as severe in this scenario compared to if they hadn't been out front of the problem? I know that I would be less severe, thus reinforcing the benefit of proactive action.

■ **SALES EFFORTS SHOULD REPRESENT COMPANY VALUES AND ADHERE TO ASSOCIATED POLICIES.**
While a simple concept, this is a significant challenge in business today.

One of the biggest issues I have seen is that while you may be able to control your values, you can't control those of your customers. In some cases, it may be difficult to obtain work because of the values gap.

Two of the biggest values gaps I have seen involve the exploitation of women and *'kick backs' (whether money or gifts/perks)*. Virtually all companies have values or policies that prohibit the exploitation of women and 'kick backs'. The variable is their willingness and ability to enforce these policies vary significantly (*this occurs with both vendor and customer companies*). The result is that the companies with inadequate controls end up with an under-the-radar perversion of their sales processes.

Bridging the Gap

Leadership Style: Democratic

The democratic leadership style may also be known as the participative leadership style or shared leadership style. It is characterized by employees participating more in the decision-making process.

When a democratic leader is in the process of making a decision, often many (*if not all*) team employees are requested to give input and participate in the process.

Democratic leaders will often select employees to participate that share their principles and beliefs.

Other criteria for selection may include honesty, competency, work ethic, creativity, and a specialty skillset.

During the decision-making process, the democratic leader may act more as a facilitator than the decision maker (*however the leader does retain the final decision authority*).

The advantages of the democratic leadership style are:

- **CREATIVE SOLUTIONS.**
  Decisions from a democratic leader tend to include thoughts and ideas from a number of employees. These varied contributions can lead to more refined and innovative decisions.

- **INVOLVEMENT AND COMMITMENT.**
  When employees are given the opportunity to contribute to a decision, they usually take more ownership in the decision. This ownership tends to improve their involvement and commitment to success.

Disadvantages of the democratic leadership style are:

- **INEFFICIENCY.**
  The democratic leader's process of employee selection, employee input, and then making the decision hinders their ability to make timely decisions. In situations where not all employees participate in the decision, there can be breakdowns in communicating the decision to all employees.

- **DISENFRANCHISED EMPLOYEES.**
  Democratic leaders may exclude employees from the decision-making process for valid reasons such as lack of knowledge or expertise. They may also allow a personal bias to influence the employee selection process. Regardless, when employees are not selected by the leader to provide decision input, they can have lower morale and performance.

Democratic leaders are most successful in environments with highly competent employees that share a strong, cohesive bond with each other and the leader.

"If an employee's elemental need to feel safe from workplace bullying and violence isn't met, then your improvement efforts will not be successful."

– TIM MARSH

Chapter 15:

Learning the Hard Way

"To be successful as an employee or leader, you have to develop personal discipline, filters, and self-control to resist destructive impulses."

– TIM MARSH

Contemplations:

- *Have you ever worked for a supervisor that obviously didn't like you? How could you tell? Did you know why? How did this affect your job results, performance, and satisfaction?*

- *Recall a time you have issued 'tough love' to someone. Could it have been considered horseplay? Did it result in the intended result? Were the results long-lasting? Did you receive any consequences?*

Mind the Gap

THE LEADER HAS DECIDED TO ADD
"WHAT SHOULD WE DO?" TO THE PARKING LOT.

The Story...
Location: Oklahoma

I'd just spent months preparing for and passing my general field engineer exam. The eight-hour oral exam was the culmination of about three years of progression through the field engineer training program.

Shortly after becoming a general field engineer, I became the eastern US product champion for a specialty tool service. In this role, I was responsible for as overseeing tool inventory, maintenance, personnel training, and assisting with performing the service in the field.

PROFESSIONAL BACKSTORY: The specialty service was a tool that essentially perform ed an MRI (*magnetic resonance image*) type measurement of rock in wellbores.

The measurement was then used to ascertain the porosity of the rock (*this is the amount of space within a rock available to hold liquids or gas*), water saturation (*a scientific way of saying how much water is in the porosity versus hydrocarbon*), and how much of the water was bound to the rock by surface tension (*in this case the higher, the better*).

As part of the process to generate the measurements, the tools used magnets to polarize the hydrogen atoms in the porosity fluids (*as you can imagine, these magnets were enormously powerful*).

The powerful tool magnets would cause the internal components of a mechanical watch (*one that has gears and widgets on the inside*) to become magnetized and stop moving. They could demagnetize the credit cards in your wallet if you were to get close. They were so powerful that we could not allow any employees with pacemakers near the unshielded magnets. Due to these risks, magnetic safety training was an important part of my role.

In one of the districts, there was a field engineer, Abdul, that I had been training to perform the service. He consistently would disregard the magnetic safety precautions and operational best practices. This could not only negatively affect him, but others that might unsuspectingly walk into the area where the tool was set up.

Closing the Gap

LEADERSHIP TIP 15:

Strive to be respected, treat your employees as individuals, and take time to gain commitment.

One day, while working on the tool, I asked Abdul if he had his wallet on him. As expected, he said yes. While this was not a safety issue per se, it was a best practice not to have credit cards near the tool as it could demagnetize the strip (*in that day and time credit cards did not have RF chips, so the magnetic strip was necessary to prevent having to key in the number for every purchase*). Frustrated that he continually disregarded safety precautions and operational best practices, I asked him to see it and then laid it down on one of the tool's magnets.

Needless to say, I thought it was Hilarious, however he was not happy with me. The next day, when my manager found out what I had done, he wasn't impressed with my antics.

After another incident of him disregarding the safety precautions, I decided to teach him a lesson. I asked Abdul to lay his finger on one of the tool magnets. I then took a metal spanner wrench and brought it close to the tool. As expected, the strong magnetic field attracted the wrench, causing it to smash into his finger. I actually thought that the impact had broken his finger. I knew he was hurt bad when tears came to his eyes.

I immediately regretted what I'd done. I could just see myself getting fired for this little stunt. Luckily for me, his finger wasn't broken. In retrospect, I now realize that all of these tough love incidents were often nothing but a variant of horseplay.

These aren't the only incidents of tough love that I have used over the years. Some were not near as bad, while some were likely much worse. While these methods may have worked, I can now see the human cost of my actions.

...and the Lessons Learned:

- **CONSIDER THE HUMAN COST.**

  What I mean by this is whenever you are making important decisions, from personnel matters to purchasing equipment, it is wise counsel to pause to reflect on their implications.

  When decisions affect people positively, these are no-brainers. Leaders will gain goodwill and better overall results by consistently erring on the side of the employees' benefit.

  Tougher are the decisions that affect one or more employees in a negative way. In these cases, such as terminating an underperforming employee who may be a friend or have a large family, it can be gut-wrenching. While it is advisable to pause and reflect to ensure you have done the necessary due diligence, there is a balance, as excessive delays only serve to compound the difficulty.

- **IT ONLY TAKES A FEW SECONDS TO UNDO SIGNIFICANT EFFORTS.**

  In the example given, my off-the-cuff decision to use the spanner wrench to teach a lesson had the potential not only to break his finger, but to undo several years' worth of my hard work with the company. In retrospect, I can't believe that I allowed a tough love lesson to jeopardize my ability to provide for my family.

  While seemingly harmless, leaders can't condone horse-play. Countless examples attest to how playful banter can quickly turn into an accident or injury.

To be successful as an employee or leader, you have to develop personal discipline, filters, and self-control to resist destructive impulses. This lesson learned not only applies to business, but equally applies to your personal life.

Bridging the Gap
Leadership Style: Servant

A servant leadership style is characterized by the leader's desire to put their people before their power. While this may seem simple, despite having a strong commitment, it can be challenging (*especially if it isn't your natural leadership style*).

There are a number of principles common among servant leaders:

- **SELF-REALIZATION OF LIMITATIONS AND STRENGTHS.**
  It's important to know your team. It's equally important to self-reflect on your own limitations and strengths. By understanding yourself, opportunities for self-improvement and to utilize the strengths of others become more apparent.

- **LISTENING TO EMPLOYEES.**
  Servant leaders listen intently, without interruption, and with their full attention to their employees. Taking the time to listen to employees conveys you care about them and what they have to say.

- **LEADING BY EXAMPLE.**
  Leaders that are willing to do any task that they would ask their employees to do tend to build creditability and trust. This stewardship is essential for a well-rounded and functional team.

- **EMPLOYEE DEVELOPMENT.**
  Servant leaders care about the development and growth of their employees. They know that these are critical to their employee's success and long-term satisfaction.

- **CONTINUOUS IMPROVEMENT.**
  Monitoring, assessing, and continuous improvement (*whether quality, safety, profitability, etc.*) is paramount to servant leaders.

- **GIVING BACK TO THE COMMUNITY.**
  Servant leaders understand and lead knowing that one of the benefits of a successful business is the ability to give back to local communities.

- **CONSENSUS BUILDING.**
  While not democratic with decision-making, the servant leadership style does seek to build team consensus with decisions. In the event consensus is not possible, they will usually take the action with the greatest benefit to the overall team and company.

- **STRATEGIC PLANNING.**
  Taking the lessons learned today and ensuring they are implemented to improve future operations is typical for the servant leadership style. They understand, prioritize, and improve the company for everyone's benefit.

- **EMPATHY.**
  A servant leader knows and cares about their employees. This translates beyond work to their families and interests outside of work. Servant leaders understand that caring is an essential component of empathy (*and sympathy*).

- **REHABILITATION AND RESTORATION.**
Many employees are carrying current or past workplace trauma. Whether a hostile relationship with a manager or co-worker or some form of harassment, this trauma is detrimental to them both personally and professionally. A servant leader assists their employees with rehabilitation and restoration.

"The expectations of professionalism at work varies widely in business today."

– TIM MARSH

Chapter 16:

Enabled Undermining

"Succession planning is key to continuing operations when an essential person either becomes unavailable or leaves the company."

– TIM MARSH

Contemplations:

- *Recall a time in which your authority was undermined. What factors enabled it to occur? How did the situation get resolved? Were there long-term consequences?*

- *Consider a time in which someone who was critical to the company resigned. Did the departure result in a large disruption in the business? How long was it until the business returned to the same level as before they left?*

Mind the Gap

BOB IS WORRIED ABOUT VIOLATING
THE CHAIN OF COMMAND.

The Story...

Location: Pennsylvania

This lesson is of particular importance as it highlights some of my worst personnel decisions. In hindsight, I let myself enable an employee to undermine his manager to the point in which he resigned (*before I was about to terminate him*).

Before I get ahead of myself, let me start from the beginning.

I had just taken over an operation that consisted of seven locations and spanned Illinois to Pennsylvania to Virginia.

Many of the employees and the entire management had lots of seniority. There was very little management bench strength to take over once the existing management team either moved on to other positions or retired.

Case in point was in the largest district and former headquarters. The field service manager had over twenty years of seniority. He had been moved into his current position more from the basis of his seniority and the need to move him out of the rigorous field position versus qualification for the job. While deeply competent in field operations, he was not a strong operations manager. The organizational structure was designed to minimize cost, thus there were limited positions outside of the field operations.

Closing the Gap

LEADERSHIP TIP 16:

Embrace failure, be your own toughest critic, and step up in times of crisis.

I wanted to grow the business, improve quality, and increase competency. To do this, I already knew that we needed to add a couple staff positions to help facilitate these goals. The field service manager was a good fit for the technical position I had in mind.

His position was one that we wanted to fill internally. In an organization that had limited opportunities for advancement, going to the outside would have frustrated the people.

Since there was no single obvious candidate for the job, I decided to post the position. Six engineers in the location (*essentially every engineer*) applied for the job. Rather than simply interviewing the candidates and deciding, I felt that we needed to take a better look at their leadership skills before filling this critical role. I decided to give each candidate a two-week opportunity to work in the position. This would give me time to see how they were able to handle the stresses and responsibilities. This exercise narrowed the field down to two candidates (*four engineers rescinded their application once they experienced the position*).

To complicate matters, one of the remaining candidates (*and I felt the best candidate*) was the son of one of the former owners. In the old organization, he would have been the default choice. Not so in the new company, which made my position complicated. If I promoted him, the employees would see it as me pacifying the other former owners (*all of whom were managers in one form or fashion in the company*). If I didn't promote him, I would not be making the best decision for the company.

In the end, I promoted the engineer who was the best candidate for the job. Although I had not been in the position long, I felt that most who knew anything about me would know that right or wrong, my decision would be what I thought was best for the company irrespective of his ties to the former owners.

This whole experience left one lasting lesson learned. In an operation of our size, it is critical that succession planning be in place in order to avoid gaps when key personnel change positions or leave the company.

As a result, I decided to start identifying high-potential engineers in each of my locations that we could start grooming for future support and management positions.

There was a particularly talented engineer that was identified as high-potential. I had seen this for myself, independent of the assessment by his manager.

Eager to fast track some of the high-potential candidates, I got personally involved with their training, development, and mentoring. This was the case with this engineer. As a result, the engineer and I started communicating regularly regarding his development.

In retrospect, the engineer had some challenges I didn't initially see. The biggest being that he was overly eager to be promoted through whatever means. His eagerness to be promoted (*at the time, there wasn't any open positions*) combined with my eagerness to develop my bench strength ultimately led to me making a series of bad decisions.

PERSONAL BACKSTORY: A poor personnel decision was when I allowed a mentoring relationship to migrate to a direct line of communication. This allowed him to begin circumventing his manager. Now, instead of developing his skills, he was (*unfortunately*) manipulating the situation to advance his personal agenda of displacing his manager.

I was getting one-sided information that resulted in me unfairly developing opinions on the skills and competency of the manager without giving him the benefit of rebuking the claims and assertions.

In the end, I did take action to remove the manager (*not entirely based on the actions of the engineer that was sabotaging him*) to another position in the company. While it was not portrayed to him as a demotion, he immediately saw it for what it was. It didn't take long for him to leave the company.

The irony (*and perhaps justice*) of the situation was that the engineer was not promoted to replace the manager. At the time, I remember thinking that he would have been a good replacement candidate if he only had some more development time. So, in the end, the engineer's efforts were unsuccessful. His desired outcome occurred (*his manager leaving*); however, it occurred too quickly for him to benefit.

Without a qualified candidate, I had to go outside the organization to fill the manager position. In the end, the engineer left the company, having never again been promoted.

...and the Lessons Learned:

- **SUCCESSION PLANNING IS CRITICAL TO PREVENT OPERATIONAL DISRUPTIONS.** Succession planning is key to continuing operations when an essential person either becomes unavailable (*such as an extended sickness*) or leaves the company.

  One common mistake I have seen repeatedly is when leaders (*or owners*) think that succession planning in smaller companies is less critical than larger companies (*the misconception is that as the number of employees increase, so does the importance*). Succession planning in a smaller company is of utmost important due to the fewer number of potential employees that can fill gaps.

  Unfortunately, with many leaders, regardless of company size, the first time they think of succession planning is when they need it most. As a result, they suffer from either working without an essential position filled or rush to fill the position (*often with a less than ideal candidate*).

  In the best case scenario, all essential personnel will have succession candidates identified within the company or a plan of action if it is required to go outside to recruit a replacement. Having this preparatory work done in advance allows leaders to better handle the other effects of personnel changes.

- **ORGANIZATIONAL CHAIN-OF-COMMAND IS IMPORTANT.**

This single lesson learned is very important. I have seen numerous examples (*including my own*) of where not following it has led to serious problems.

Leaders and employees may not follow the chain-of-command (COC) for a variety of reasons. These happen from the top down and bottom up.

In cases of top down, leaders or owners usually skip one or more levels of management to get something done or obtain information. They justify these COC breaches since the employee is in their reporting structure or because they own the company. Regardless of the justification, and while not always negative, routinely circumventing the COC is harmful for organizational discipline.

Leaders or owners that feel the need to consistently bypass the COC may want to consider flattening their organizational chart to eliminate management layers.

In the cases of bottom up, leaders need to create an environment where employees are not intimidated or uncomfortable speaking with them, while at the same time maintaining COC. Therefore, it is critical that leaders understand the purpose of discussions outside the COC. Upon determining the discussion purpose (*this obviously doesn't include appropriate purely social interactions*), leaders need to either encourage employees to follow the COC or become involved if the situation warrants (*such as when an issue with the employee's direct manager is the subject*).

Bridging the Gap
Leadership Style: Pacesetter

The pacesetter leadership style can be best described by the phrase "do as I do, now". It's characterized by high expectations from the leader that everyone on their team works with at least the same pace as them (*with equal or better quality and performance*).

These are some common traits of the pacesetter leadership style:

- **MOTIVATION EXPECTATIONS.**
  A pacesetter leader is highly self-motivated and expects the same from each member of their team. Their self-motivation stems from a strong desire to succeed. A pacesetter leader is hyper driven to achieve results.

- **COMMUNICATION.**
  The pacesetter leadership style relies on unambiguous communication between the leader and team members.

- **EFFICIENCY.**
  The pacesetter leadership style is preoccupied with time and efficiency. The leaders are always seeking ways to get more done in less time.

- **LEAD BY EXAMPLE.**
  The pacesetter leader is the role model who they want all of their team members to emulate. Team members that can't perform at the leader's standards are typically removed or replaced.

The advantages of the pacesetter leadership style are:

- The leader's continuous focus on efficiency improvements results in quick remedies to problems and concerns.

- Results from teams with a pacesetter leader tend to be on time and high quality.

- Team members tend to be highly competent.

Disadvantages of the pacesetter leadership style are:

- Keeping up with the leader's pace can lead to employee stress and feeling overwhelmed.

- Since substandard employees are removed or replaced, pacesetter leaders tend to give the remaining employees little or no feedback.

- Over time, employees may become demotivated and disengaged.

"A common pitfall with discipline in many companies is the inequities that occur"

– TIM MARSH

"Whenever you see a successful business, someone once made a courageous decision."

– Peter Drucker

Chapter 17:

The Heart Patient

"The flawed leadership traits that allow a company to revert back to failed policies and procedures are those that will prevent a leader from leading to prosperity."

– Tim Marsh

Contemplations:

- *Recall a time in which you worked for a leader who was dismissive of obvious regulatory compliance issues. Why do you think they ignored them? What was the severity of the risk?*

- *Have you ever been subject to a regulatory compliance inspection? What were the results? Were they unexpected? What actions took place in response? Were these actions sustained long-term?*

"NURSE, DO YOU MIND HANDING
ME ONE OF THOSE DONUTS?"

The Story...

Location: ██████████ (*Redacted*)

It is common to hear stories about heart patients who survive a major incident (*such as a heart attack or open-heart surgery*) and go on to change their diet and introduce exercise into their routine, only to revert back to their old ways.

All too often, this same behavior pattern occurs in business. Companies survive a major or catastrophic incident only to revert to the actions that led to the incident. They either didn't learn from their past lessons, or worse, failed to act on the lessons they have learned.

In my career, I have unfortunately seen this numerous times. The incidents span the spectrum with respect to incident type, with the most common involving finance, people, and regulatory compliance.

While many incidents I witnessed weren't regulatory compliance related, the ones involving finance and people are too complicated or involve too many personal details to effectively discuss in this format. Regardless, all of the incident types have common threads that I will illustrate with the following examples.

At one point, I was working for a company that shared common ownership with a number of other companies. As such, while not an official employee of all the companies, I was often called upon by all the companies to assist with tasks in which I am competent.

Such was the case when I was handed a letter that one of the affiliate companies received from the state regarding the company's air pollution permit.

Prior to me coming aboard, the state had audited the company's operations and found a number of violations. Typically, these violations result in a notice of violation letter and a fine. The state's expectations were that the company corrects the violations and pay the fine. After a short period, the state usually follows up to ensure the violations have been corrected and the company's operations continue with the corrections.

In this case, the company's safety representative received the letter regarding the violations. He simply placed the letter in the file and carried on with business as usual. As is often the case, the safety duties were only one portion of the employee's job. To complicate the matter, few people in the company (*including the owners*) were overly interested in compliance. This approach was likely the result of never having any previous compliance issues (*with any regulatory agency*) despite operating in violation for years, perhaps decades.

Now I am back to when I was given the state's letter regarding the company's air pollution permit. In the letter, it spelled out the lack of response from the company and the proposed action on the part of the state, which included the possibility of suspending or cancelling the permit.

It was at this point that I found out about the previous letter in the file and really began to understand the owners' mindset regarding compliance.

Having worked with state and federal air quality compliance officials for over a decade, I set forth to contain and mitigate the lack of response and the original violations.

After successfully navigating a resolution with the state, I sat down with the owners to discuss the many other areas of non-compliance I had observed. Not surprisingly, I was met with a general unwillingness to address the issues.

In the time since my compliance conversation, the company has faced multiple non-compliance incidents (*and they continue to have tremendous regulatory exposure*). These incidents came at a high cost, with little long-term benefits beyond getting past the immediate crisis. Only time will tell whether they learned the lessons from all of these incidents.

At another point in my career, I worked for a company where I received a call one day from an ATF investigator. He proceeded to tell me that one of our employees had called and filed a complaint about the explosive operations at one of our locations.

The investigator let me know that the ATF Area Director would be following up the conversation with a letter summarizing the complaint as well as the expected response and timeline for the company.

Closing **the Gap**

LEADERSHIP TIP 17:

Link results with goals. Give appreciation and rewards.

As you can imagine, this is not the type of phone call anyone wants to receive. The ramifications are even more problematic when you know there is validity to the multitude of potential violations at the company. Having never had any negative ATF contact, management was caught off guard and very concerned. Personally, I was glad that the complaint was limited in scope. I knew a full-scale inspection of the explosive operations would uncover numerous violations (*one of the reasons I was brought onboard was to resolve these problematic areas*). It would be catastrophic for the company.

As a result of the call, as expected, all priority was put on addressing the specific complaints made. Money became no object and resources were made available. In the end, the complaint areas were identified and resolved.

I submitted the paperwork to the ATF documenting the actions that were taken. The response to our significant and impressive efforts was positive, and the case was resolved. Management was relieved and, for a short period supported addressing the large number of remaining potential violations.

In time, however, this commitment faded and the operations went back to normal. I subsequently left the company. I am told by former colleagues that they have more potential violations now than at the time prior to the initial phone call.

...and the Lessons Learned:

- **THE 3 AFTERMATH ACCEPTANCE PHASES OF A CATASTROPHIC BUSINESS EVENT.**

  ### Proactive
  This acceptance phase is represented by leaders (*or owners*) not only resolving the immediate catastrophic event, but also actively seeking out and addressing any known or new issue that may lead to a future catastrophic incident.

  ### Selective
  This acceptance phase is characterized by leaders (*or owners*) resolving the immediate catastrophic event; however, minimal effort is given to seeking out new or addressing any known issue that may lead to a future catastrophic event.

  ### Dismissive
  This acceptance phase is characterized by the passive or blatantly aggressive response to the catastrophic event. In some cases, the event is not fully resolved (*and often the consequences exasperated*) due to the response. Ignorance, blame, and denial are the hallmark responses of leaders (*or owners*).

- **FAILURE TO LEARN FROM YOUR MISTAKES RESULTS FROM INCOMPETENCE OR GROSS NEGLIGENCE.**
  It's an ineffective leader that does not learn from the mistakes of others. It's an incompetent leader that doesn't learn from one's own mistakes. Beyond that, any lessons when it comes to safety rise to the level of gross negligence.

The flawed leadership traits that allow a company to revert to failed policies and procedures are those that will prevent a leader (*or owner*) from leading to prosperity (*the challenge is that incompetence can't identify incompetence*).

Any company led by people with these traits can't experience substantial improvement without outside influence.

Therefore, if you work for such a company (*and are not able to be the necessary outside influence*), regardless of your current circumstances or upside potential, it is prudent to seek other opportunities.

Bridging the Gap
Leadership Style: Visionary

It's possible to be a visionary without being in a leadership role. It's also possible to be in a leadership role without being a visionary. A visionary leader is a person who sees things differently. Rather than simply looking at the status quo and seeing opportunities to make it better, they look at it and see how they can make it different (*hopefully in beneficial ways*).

The advantages of the visionary leadership style are:

- Visionary leaders understand and seek to instill the company's mission and values in the opportunities they envision.

- Effective visionary leaders are able to communicate their vision and obtain buy in from leadership and employees.

- Visionary leaders can bring innovative ideas to stagnant businesses that can reinvigorate them.

Disadvantages of the visionary leadership style are:

- By focusing on the 10,000' big picture, visionary leaders may miss important day-to-day details.

- Leaders with a visionary leadership style may sacrifice current performance and results by focusing on too much on future opportunities.

- Visionary leaders may overlook better opportunities because of their intense focus on an existing one.

"Combining two companies with vastly different cultures usually proves to be exceedingly difficult. Often, integration problems and resistance will plague the merged company long into the future."

– Tim Marsh

Chapter 18:

Expect vs Inspect

"Whether intentional or not, often the first question asked about any topic during an inquiry or investigation gets the ole 'management head fake'."

– Tim Marsh

Contemplations:

- *Recall a time when you were told one thing but discovered the opposite to be true. What caused the discrepancy? What impact did the discrepancy have on your business?*

- *Have you ever performed an investigation where you were intentionally misled? What motivated the attempt to mislead? What were the consequences? Were you able to determine the actual root causes?*

"I THINK WE'LL BE PROFITABLE IF WE DO MORE JOBS."

The Story...

Location: West Virginia

PERSONAL BACKSTORY: If you are like me when I was growing up, cleaning your room consisted of throwing your dirty (*and clean if it was on the floor*) laundry in the hamper and throwing the rest of the stuff on your floor into drawers and your closet. The result was a room that looked clean upon a cursory glance, but upon further inspection, was not.

It didn't take my mom long to figure out my game. She then started to inspect more thoroughly whenever she asked me to clean my room. Likewise, it didn't take me long to realize that it wasn't worth the risk, as she would usually empty the entire drawer or closet in the middle of my bedroom floor when she found my stuff hidden there.

In business, many of the lessons I learned as a child still hold true. The old adage, "people do what you inspect, not what you expect" still applies today (*perhaps more than ever*).

I had recently taken over an operations position after having been in support (*technical and safety*) for several years. The operation appeared sound from the outside. The financial results were good, the safety record was above average, and customer contracts renewed year after year. I really didn't have any reason to question the core behaviors, but my gut told me that if we were going to take this business to the next level, we were going to have to make sure the foundation was solid. My gut, that little voice inside, was telling me that I needed to dig a little deeper.

My first step was to evaluate the people. Regardless of how good your financial position, your equipment, or your market share, it is a rare business whose success is not dominated by the people involved.

I had been on service jobs we provided and was satisfied with the overall execution. It was only after I started asking questions that I saw the deficiencies in the competencies of our people and the short-comings of many of our personnel policies and procedures. Although concerned, I was confident that we could overcome these deficiencies. Once we did, our people were ready to take us to the that next level.

The next step was to evaluate our equipment and operation policies and procedures. For this exercise, I gathered all of my best support and operations people to have a surprise audit at our largest facility *(which was also the flagship location for the area)*.

Closing the Gap

LEADERSHIP TIP 18:

Don't be static in a comfort zone. Instead, seek to be comfortable working in a dynamic environment.

The surprise on everyone's face was obvious when I walked in and told the crews to pull every piece of equipment off their trucks.

At that point, I ask the safety manager to inspect each truck for the required paper-work and safety equipment. To go the extra step and ensure all the paperwork was up to date and the safety equipment was functional and within calibration.

I asked the area mechanic to go through all the trucks and support vehicles. Check the fluid levels, tire pressures, and thoroughly inspect all the items that are part of a routine pre-trip inspection.

I asked our area electronics technician to look at all the tools on the trucks to make sure they were within calibration and had the proper auxiliary equipment installed. He also ensured all the fluid levels in the tools were correct and that the required equipment to maintain and operate the tools was available on the truck. The electronics technician then turned his attention to the computer and acquisition system to ensure the system was fully operational, calibrated, and that the latest software updates were installed.

I asked our service quality manager to thoroughly go through data sets from each crew to ensure we were following our operating procedures and the customer's requirements.

I asked our operations management to go through the district equipment not assigned to a truck to make sure that it was maintained and available. This included backup tools and calibration equipment. We then inspected all the required postings and evaluated the overall operations to ensure compliance with company policies and procedures.

Essentially, the inspection was a comprehensive look at the district operations as well as that of each individual crew. In some areas, I was pleasantly surprised as our performance was outstanding. Unfortunately, my gut was correct in many areas, as we were woefully underperforming. As expected, some crews really struggled, while others excelled. In general, regardless of the level of performance, the entire experience turned out to be positive for the district. Those who were subpar improved their game. Those who were outstanding finally got recognition for their efforts.

One of the primary reasons that the results were positive was due to how we handled the issues found. Rather than hand out discipline and criticism, we embraced the changes that needed to be made and supported those who needed to make them. We gave rewards to the outstanding crews (*at all levels, not just the leaders*). In this supportive environment, we achieved the progress sought.

...and the Lessons Learned:

■ **THE FOLLOW-UP QUESTIONS USUALLY GIVE THE BEST INCITES WHEN TRYING TO PROBE FOR ADDITIONAL INFORMATION.**
Whether intentional or not, often the first round of questions asked during an inquiry or investigation usually gets the ole 'management head fake'. By this, I mean the response is what they think you want to hear. In this scenario, the focus is on positive results, with problems vaguely mentioned and then smoothed over.

An inexperienced leader will accept these platitudes and move on. With more experience, leaders learn that the complete details are normally revealed by asking the follow-up second, third, or more questions.

■ **POSITIVE RESULTS ARE MORE LIKELY TO OCCUR IN A SUPPORTIVE ENVIRONMENT.**
So many times, I have seen where managers (*note that I didn't say leaders*) become irate when there are issues. I've never seen this type of hostile environment work to resolve a situation or prevent reoccurrence.

On the flip side, I've seen calm, measured responses have the exact opposite result. In this supportive environment, people are encouraged to identify, plan, and correct the issues without fear of reprisals. The ability to learn helps to avoid repeating the issue.

This isn't to say there are no consequences or disciplinary actions taken in a supportive environment. Quite the contrary. The primary difference however is the motivation of the leader. In a supportive environment, consequences and disciplinary actions are used to develop and guide the employee rather than as a punishment. This subtle difference in motivation leads to significantly more positive results.

Bridging the Gap
Leadership Style: Transformational

The transformational leadership style relies upon employee inspiration and motivation to facilitate the desired changes. The leaders and employees sharpen the performance and results of each other.

Benefits of this leadership style are:

- Higher employee morale

- Improved creativity and innovation

- Increased job satisfaction and lower turnover

- Higher employee loyalty and commitment

Transformational leadership is characterized by:

- Respect and responsibility for self and others

- Inspiring innovation and creativity

- Promoting fairness and integrity

- Providing employee encouragement, recognition, and support

- Effective communication of goals and objectives to team members

- Having an inspirational vision for their team

- Strong self-awareness

- Inspiring employees to change

Mind the Gap:

Leadership Basics III

Team Resources and Support

A leader that has built a team of highly effective, quality employees understands that without sufficient resources and adequate support, the team will not be able to achieve their maximum potential.

While common resources may vary widely, they include:

- Financial
- Leadership support
- Training materials and classes
- Safety equipment
- Operational tools and equipment
- Parts and supplies
- Documentation

Support department examples include:

- Human resources
- Quality, health, safety, and environment
- Accounting
- Legal
- Information technology
- Sales and marketing

Employee Motivation

It is important to understand that with employee motivation it is easier to hire motivated people and then not demotivate them than the opposite where you are trying to inspire unmotivated people.

Employee motivation is affected by a multitude of distinct factors and you must strive to understand all of them.

One common factor is that high-quality, talented, and motivated employees do not want to the burden of others who are not.

Your ability to manage employee motivation factors is key to closing personnel gaps and releasing your employees' untapped potential.

Business Plans

A business plan is an effective method to communicate goals and objectives to your employees (keep in mind that the scope of your business plan may range from an individual team to the entire company).

A typical business plan includes some or all of the following topics:

- Mission and vision statements
- Scope and purpose
- Competitor SWOT analyses
- Company organizational structure
- Sales and marketing targets, assignments, and timelines
- Operational resources and support
- Personnel objectives
- Financial performance metrics, KPIs, and results assessment
- Auditing and continuous improvement mechanisms

Employee Retention

While pay and benefits are one reason that an employee may choose to look for other employment opportunities, all too often, employees are also seeking other non-financial priorities such as career development and advancement opportunities, respect, appreciation, high-quality colleagues, and challenging work tasks.

An effective performance bonus program can increase employee retention. These performance bonuses may be periodic (quarterly, annual, etc.) or discretionary.

Periodic performance bonuses are usually higher award amounts and are tied to a documented set of objectives. Discretionary bonuses are normally not tied to any specific goals and objectives. As with performance bonuses, periodic discretionary bonuses are frequently larger amounts. Instant discretionary bonuses are given as an immediate reward for action or performance. Even though these are typically smaller amounts, they are quite effective in demonstrating appreciation to your employees.

Company retention programs that combine compensation, financial and non-financial benefits, improved job satisfaction opportunities, and workplace flexibility are the most successful. A particularly effective program is one that combines career development with compensation increases for merit and progression milestones.

Punctuality and Attendance

Expectations for punctuality and attendance vary significantly in business today. Regardless of what expectations you have for punctuality and attendance, they need to be clearly defined, communicated, and equally enforced.

While some job functions (such as delivery drivers, plumbers, and emergency response personnel) require punctuality and attendance in order to sustain productivity, meet client needs, or prevent havoc, many other job functions have the flexibility to forego such rigorous expectations. Despite having flexibility, many leaders find themselves stuck in the mid-twentieth century mentality of requiring their employees to come to work every day, punch the clock, and work forty hours per week.

With the technology available to the modern workforce, it's often more advantageous to focus on efficiency, performance, and results.

Company Culture

There are a number of traits and characteristics you can associate with developing a high performance company culture. These include:

- High-quality, competent employees that strive for continuous improvement and development
- Empowered leadership and employees
- High job satisfaction and low employee attrition
- Leader and employee accountable for individual performance and overall results

- Candor, trust, integrity, and mechanisms to manage conflict
- Utilizing the competencies and skillsets of all employees
- Clarity and focus on company mission and discipline to adhere to strategic focus

Promotions for the Wrong Reasons

When promoting from within, leaders who select a candidate for the wrong reasons (such as comfort level, friendship, inappropriate relationship, etc.) will undoubtedly face challenges in the future.

While this may not seem like a significant issue, eventually the ramifications will become evident and adversely impact the business.

The decision to promote an employee for the wrong reasons will demotivate high-quality employees (including any who were qualified for the position along with those who work with the newly promoted employee).

Healthy Competition

Creating a work environment where teams or individual employees work in healthy competition with each other can lead to better results, higher morale, and increased job satisfaction.

A key to creating healthy competition is to ensure the reward for winning is appropriate. An appropriate healthy competition reward is a trophy or other recognition.

When the competition reward becomes too valuable or coveted, the intended healthy competition can cross the line into counterproductive competitive behaviors. Large cash bonuses or high value prizes are examples of this type of reward.

"To be successful, you have to have your heart in your business, and your business in your heart."

– THOMAS WATSON

Chapter 19:

A Decision Already Made

"By gaining buy-in from employees on critical decisions, leaders not only take advantage of getting multiple viewpoints, but also have the opportunity to immediately address any resistance and dissention."

– TIM MARSH

Contemplations:

- *Recall a time when you made a poor decision because you were closed-minded. What caused you to disregard any other alternatives? What impact did it have?*

- *Have you ever been unwilling to consider an alternative? How did this impact you? Do you think the outcome would have changed, had you considered an alternative?*

BOB CAME BACK FROM THE LAS VEGAS LEADERSHIP
CONFERENCE WITH LOTS OF NEW IDEAS.

The Story...

Location: Canada

PERSONAL BACKSTORY: Living and working in Canada was a fun and exciting experience for me. I enjoyed meeting new people, seeing new things, and living in a place that was similar to the US but just slightly different. Canada offered all the benefits of living in a foreign country, without the culture shock. It was a great *first living out of the country* experience.

Working in Canada was also different. Many of the areas in northern Alberta where I was working was remote, uninhabited, and generally not accessible outside of the winter months when the ground was frozen and ice roads could be constructed.

For me, the concept of a road made out of ice was baffling. My whole life, I had tried to avoid icy roads. Governments spent millions of dollars on road plows, salt, and other chemicals trying to rid the winter roads of ice, and now I was living where they intentionally built roads made of ice. Not only did the roads get built out of ice, but also ice bridges were commonplace.

The district I was managing spanned much of northeastern Alberta and included many of these annual winter projects. To put it into perspective, to drive north to south of the district would have taken approximately sixteen hours while east to west was about half of that.

We had ten trucks assigned to the district, of which we crewed between two and four during the non-winter months. During the winter, we operated twenty-four trucks. The additional trucks, crews, and equipment came from all parts of the world. Conveniently, the winter is slow in many areas, so resources were readily available.

Needless to say, organizing the movement of all of these trucks, equipment, and lining out the crew members was a major undertaking that took two months of preparation every year.

Fortunate for me, I had Bob, who was a senior field engineer that had been commandeered by my predecessor into more of a field service manager role. He had assisted with this process for a number of years and was to be my go-to guy for the winter projects.

Witty and smart, Bob had a typical laid back personality of many of his countrymen. Content with the role he was in, he was not overly career ambitious. As a result, Bob was extremely delinquent on his progression to general field engineer.

About a month into our preparations for the winter projects, I received a call from my manager that Clyde (*his manager who ran all of the Canadian product line operations*) wanted to meet with us. I had met Clyde a number of times and had a good relationship with him. Curious as to the purpose of the meeting, but not overly concerned, I traveled to Calgary. When I walked into Clyde's office, Sam (*my manager*) was already there.

After some brief small talk, Clyde told me, "I'm terminating Bob. Now what are we going to do?" I was taken aback. "Why?" I asked. At the end of the day, there had been an edict from corporate to purge the organization of engineers that were severely delinquent in the company's progression program. I resisted. I reminded Clyde that we were square in the middle of planning for the winter projects and that I didn't have the experience or expertise to do this without his assistance. I could tell that Clyde didn't like my push back. He was a small, rotund French Canadian who was quick tempered and not adept at hiding his emotions.

He said, "Don't ruin your career over a decision that's already been made." I just sat there. *Wow*, I thought. *We just put millions of dollars of revenue in jeopardy.*

I walked out of the Calgary office angry, disheartened, and frustrated beyond belief. I didn't want to make a rash decision, but really thought about resigning right then and there.

The next day I had calmed down to the point where I didn't want to resign, but my anxiety level was through the roof. Bob had been summoned to Calgary for his last meeting, and I was sitting in my office contemplating how I was going to salvage my business.

Fortunately, I had bench strength. I immediately called in Miles, who was one of my general field engineers. Tall and mature, he had been a professional basketball player in Yugoslavia in his youth. He was ambitious to grow and had experience working as an engineer during the winter projects. I promoted him to engineer-in-charge for the winter projects. Now it was time for us to regroup and carry on with the job at hand.

Closing the Gap

LEADERSHIP TIP 19:

Be genuine, be dependable, and be decisive.

The next month was brutal for both of us. We had people and equipment coming from all over the world. It may seem simple, but we literally had to teach the people from around the world how to drive on the right side of the road and use the North American telephone system. Equipment had to be winterized and prepped for the relentless pace associated with the winter projects.

Eventually, we got all everything organized and the operations got under way on time and fully prepared, but not without taking a toll.

...and the Lessons Learned:

- **HIGH LEVEL COMPANY DIRECTIVES MAY HAVE UNINTENDED CONSEQUENCES.**
  In many cases, these unintended consequences only become apparent during the execution of the directive. They are also more likely to occur as directive complexity increases and implementation flexibility given to leadership decreases.

In my case, corporate management sent out a directive that resulted in Bob losing his job. Was that the best course of action for the company? Perhaps, but I didn't think so. I think that previous management took advantage of Bob's willingness to take on the bulk of the less glamorous parts of their job such that they didn't push for him to progress. In this, they helped themselves at his expense (*there are lessons to be learned by this behavior as well*).

By the time I arrived in the district, my efforts towards helping him were too late, since I wasn't given any input in the decision to terminate his employment.

- **LEADERS SHOULD WORK TO OBTAIN EMPLOYEE BUY-IN WHEN MAKING CRITICAL DECISIONS.**
  By gaining buy-in from employees on critical decisions, leaders not only take advantage of getting multiple viewpoints (*some of which they likely have not considered*) but also have the opportunity to immediately address any resistance and dissention. In addition, employees who feel ownership in the decision process have better performance and job satisfaction.

Bridging the Gap
Leadership Style: Coaching

A coaching leader must not be confused with a coach. It's fundamentally a dynamic relationship between a leader and their employees. This relationship provides for guidance to the employee, information exchanges through conversations, and increased employee training and development.

In addition, a coaching leader ensures their employees work independently while conveying a sense of support and involvement in their work.

The advantages of the coaching leadership style are:

- Encourages responsibility and commitment in employees.

- Seeks to find opportunities to assist employees with developing themselves.

- Leaders are focused on setting goals and building relationships.

- Employees share their knowledge with the intent to grow and develop other team members.

- Communication between the leader and employees focuses more on collaboration.

- A supportive environment fosters innovative thought and creativity.

- Employees are taught to work autonomously by finding solutions to their own questions and problems.

Disadvantages of the coaching leadership style are:

- The structure in many companies makes the coaching leadership style difficult to implement.

- Missed deadlines and longer task completion times due to additional employee training and development.

- Upfront higher costs, time-consuming, and difficult to implement with unmotivated employees.

"It takes 20 years to build a reputation and five minutes to ruin it. If you think about that, you'll do things differently."

– WARREN BUFFETT

Chapter 20:

In the Trenches

"The most effective leaders have the ability to step back and evaluate challenging situations to see the multiple viewpoints."

– Tim Marsh

Contemplations:

- *Consider a time when you lost your temper at work. What was the cause? How did your actions affect the situation? Were there any long-term implications for your action?*

- *Have you ever been responsible for managing a start-up business? Was it a stand-alone business or part of an established company? Did you receive the necessary support? If the start-up was within an established company, did you encounter challenges or objections from the other operations?*

"YES, JIM, I AGREE. IF WE AVERAGE PROFITS THEN THE CAPITAL ALLOCATION WILL BE 50/50."

The Story...

Location: West Virginia

PERSONAL BACKSTORY: As is evident by now, I love old adages and analogies. One that seems fitting for this story is "you can't see the forest for the trees".

I was working as an area manager running a very profitable business when I was called by Tommy, my manager, and asked to help Nick, a colleague from another product line.

This new product line was just starting within the company, with huge amounts of capital being dedicated to the fully organic development.

Our product line had been in the area for decades and had the largest market share of any company. Our people were local and had great long-term relationships with the customers. Nick wanted to build off these relationships.

Closing the Gap

LEADERSHIP TIP 20:

Realize that your people are working to live versus living to work. They prioritize their families first and work second.

Understanding your competition is one of the easiest ways to gain a leg up in business. Therefore, KPIs should focus on ascertaining this data. Knowing the good allows you to match or exceed it, while knowing the bad allows you to avoid it while simultaneously selling against it.

I initially had several objections. In hindsight, some of these were valid, while other were petty and juvenile.

The first and biggest objection was the impact of their service quality on our relationships. The new product line performed large dollar, large impact services that if done poorly could have a significant negative impact on our customer.

I am embarrassed to admit my second objection had to do with office space. We were just moving into a new suite and I assumed that because our revenue and profits were so outstanding that our product line would get the most and best offices. When we were assigned modest but definitely not the best offices by the corporate staff (*the best went to Nick and his staff*), I was vocal in my disappointment and frustration.

My fears proved to be valid, as the new product line had serious start-up issues that plagued their service quality. They were spending enormous amounts of money and the results were dismal.

My product line on the other hand was starved for capital that was needed in order to continue ongoing operations and necessary for growth.

The arrogance of Nick exacerbated the situation. Things finally came to a head one day in a meeting with corporate management after yet another problematic job that was starting to negatively impact our customer relationships.

Nick was asking management for yet more money, people, equipment, and assistance (*whereas the money came from my budget and the assistance primarily from my people*). My heartburn came from their willingness to give him what he asked for while I was left to struggle.

I finally reached into my pocket, pulled out a dollar bill. I slammed it onto the table, telling Nick and corporate management, this more (censored) profit than you made this year, and you're wanting me to do more with less...".

It was unfortunate that at that point in my career, I still hadn't learned some basic *Business 101* concepts regarding start-ups and new business product lines.

...and the Lessons Learned:

- **CORPORATE MANAGEMENT SHOULD STRONGLY ADVOCATE FOR NEW BUSINESSES.**
The most effective leaders have the ability to step back and evaluate challenging situations to see the multiple viewpoints. Had I seen the bigger picture, I would have worked more closely with the management of the new business and our customers. This would have provided better strategic support and resources, in addition to maximizing everyone's efforts by leveraging our existing relationships.

    My shortcomings were exasperated by corporate management's failure to communicate the overall vision and their support of the new business effectively. By communicating the vision and their support, corporate management can not only inform employees, but also build excitement and enthusiasm throughout the organization for the new business.

    In addition to these internal communications, corporate management must also inform and support the new business to those stakeholders outside the organization. This serves to manage expectations and also build momentum for the new business.

- **NEW BUSINESSES SHOULD BE GIVEN EXTRAORDINARY MANAGEMENT SUPPORT AND RESOURCES.**
As with many lessons, I unfortunately learned this one later on in my career. If I have an excuse, it was that at the time I was in the trenches, I was unable to step back and see the bigger picture of what the company was trying to accomplish with adding the new product line. This reinforces the need to regularly pause and reflect on your position.

New businesses require a disproportionate amount of management support. This management support has several benefits. First, with corporate management's involvement, decisions can be made and resources allocated more quickly than in the usual management chain of command. Second, with the additional management support comes a multitude of experiences, ideas, and incites that can assist with the nuances specific to a business in its infancy.

I know now that new businesses require resources above and beyond those allocated to an established business. Whether for sales and marketing, new equipment, or any other multitude of uses, these resources can give exposure to the business as well as buy time and conveniences to overcome startup challenges.

Bridging the Gap

Leadership Style: Transactional

The transactional leadership style may also be known as managerial leadership. It focuses on the role of supervision, chain-of-command, and overall team performance. Transactional leaders don't typically seek company growth and change. They are focused on maintaining the status quo while enforcing rules and expectations (*albeit typically not expectations that they have developed*). Transactional leaders are adept at providing effective feedback that is useful for improvement.

Transactional leadership style strengths:

- **CLEAR CHAIN-OF-COMMAND.**
  With transactional leaders, chain-of-command and succession planning is clear and concise. The expectation is that employees will follow the chain-of-command structure.

- **COMMUNICATION OF INSTRUCTIONS.**
  A proficiency with communicating expectations and instructions ensures that employees know what is expected of them (*and usually additional situational contingencies*).

- **ENCOURAGES EMPLOYEE MOTIVATION.**
  Transactional leaders accomplish tasks by creating rewards and consequences for their employees. Employees that perform well are rewarded, while those with subpar performance receive consequences.

- **COST REDUCTIONS.**
  Higher levels of productivity generated by transactional leaders improve overall profitability.

- **SETTING GOALS AND OBJECTIVES.**
  Transactional leaders direct employees to accomplish short-term objectives that are in line with the company's overall mission and values.

Transactional leadership style weaknesses:

- **LACKS FLEXIBILITY.**
  Transactional leaders and their employees are bound by rules and structure. The leader must apply the rules and expectations equally among all employees.

- **SUCCESS DEPENDENT ON LEADER.**
  A transactional leader's success depends on their ability to evaluate the strengths and weaknesses of their employees, as well as to administer rewards and consequences.

- **STAGNATES INNOVATION AND CREATIVITY.**
  Transactional leaders prefer processes that are straight-forward, structured, and dependable. This preference stagnates innovation and creativity.

- **LACKS EMPATHY.**
  Since transactional leaders work within a set of bound-aries that can't be altered, there is only little room for emotion or grace.

- **REWARDS MUST OUTWEIGH CONSEQUENCES.**

  Transactional leaders must create a value proposition for each worker where the reward outweighs the conse-quences.

"Customer loyalty can be viewed as a flywheel for your sales efforts."

– TIM MARSH

Chapter 21:

Undoing Work

"In many cases, business changes that adversely affect momentum are done solely for the convenience of the new leader."

– Tim Marsh

Contemplations:

- *Have you ever had your efforts undone by someone? How did this make you feel? Did you agree with the decision to undo the work? What was the outcome? Did they regret undoing your efforts?*

- *Recall a time in which you were offered an opportunity that was 'too good to be true'. Did you accept? What was the outcome? Have you ever benefited from something that seemed 'too good to be true'? Have you ever had a negative experience with something 'too good to be true'?*

A FORMER EMPLOYEE GOT THE LAST LAUGH WHEN HE
BECAME A MILLIONAIRE WITH HIS NEW VENDING MACHINE.

The Story...
Location: Various

For the first time in my career, I was running my own district. I was intent on doing a great job and making a positive impact. The front offices were set up like many others, in that I had the corner manager's office, the sales staff were in the hallway leading up to my office, and our admin worked in a reception area near the front door. The engineers' room was an open room filled with ten or so desks and file cabinets.

The difficulty for me was that even though my office shared a wall with the engineers' room, I had to go into the shop area to access the engineers' room. It was crazy. The simple task of talking to the field engineers was made extremely inconvenient.

It was a no-brainer for me to add a door from my office into the engineer's room, so I could have easy accessibility. As the carpenter I hired tore down the wall board, he quipped that at some point there had been a door there in the past.

When I asked around to some of the more senior employees, they told me that there had been a door there in the past. Apparently, one of my predecessors did not like being interrupted by the engineers, so he had it closed off. I couldn't understand. When your job is to manage the field crews, and the engineers are the leaders of those crews, why would you not want to be able to have easy access to them?

Was I correct in undoing his work?

Was the door just an example of other things I unwittingly was undoing?

The answer turned out to be that each time a new leader came into the district, they undid much of their predecessor's work.

Upon further contemplation, I can't help but feel that the breakdown was due to a lack of shared culture and core values among the multitude of leaders that came and went through the years.

With the technology available to the modern workforce, it is more advantageous (*whenever possible*) to focus on the efficiency, performance, and results of your employees versus attendance.

Another instance where leadership undid change came more recently in my career. The owners of the company I worked for bought the "get rich quick" antics of Matt, a former employee.

The industry was coming out of yet another slowdown. I had been recruited to run the company and rebuild profitability. Within a few months, the company was finally profitable again, but the owners wanted more, and they wanted it faster.

> **PERSONAL BACKSTORY:** I am not sure how Matt who had quit and took half of the company's employees with him to form a competitor company would ever be able to get a conversation with the owners, but he did.
>
> Not only that, but he was able to convince them to rehire him (*to run the company*) with a ridiculous salary and sign-on bonus. With Matt came most of the new competitor's employees (*many of which were our former employees*).
>
> I was left completely in the dark until I received the call to tell me about Matt, my new manager.

Along with the new employees (*which nearly doubled our staff*) came more revenue and significantly more costs. These costs were magnified because of the double standards associated with the pay and perks given to the new employees. From higher salaries to tricked out vehicles, the core values and principles the company was built upon were no longer applicable.

The company started losing money immediately. The losses continued to mount. Matt's excuse for the loses was that it was due to expansion costs and would soon taper off. This excuse started getting old after a prolonged period of negative profitability.

After losing millions of dollars, one of the owners finally insisted that we address the situation. This time, the owners and I met directly and Matt (*who at the time was still my manager*) was left out of the loop. The problem was obvious, our cost structure was out of proportion to our revenue. The solution was to either increase the profitability of the jobs we were doing or lower our costs.

We had some very heated discussions in the following weeks. Matt refused to acknowledge that there was a problem. He insisted that we were running like his previous company and that they were profitable. In one meeting, I presented to the sales staff that some of the jobs we were doing for one customer was unprofitable.

Closing the Gap

LEADERSHIP TIP 21:

Understand if personnel challenges are attitude or aptitude before deciding your course of action.

The reply was that we were about to gain more jobs. When I explained that the more jobs we do, the more money we lose and that we would be more profitable not doing any jobs, the meeting turned into pandemonium. Matt couldn't and wouldn't listen to the facts and figures. He kept insisting that we should be profitable, yet we weren't.

Ultimately, almost everyone that was hired had to be released in a measure to save the company. The second month after their departure, we returned to profitability. Burdened by the legacy costs of the yearlong endeavor, the company's profitability was negatively affected long after the employees left the company.

...and the Lessons Learned:

- **Lack of shared culture and core values results in chaotic leadership transitions.**

  In many cases, business changes that adversely affect momentum are done solely for the convenience of the new leader. These changes divert time, effort, and financial resources that could be used in other areas to improve or grow the business.

  Let's use a child's toy top as an analogy for an existing business. The current leader has the top spinning with high momentum to the right. All is operating smoothly, and the leader transitions the business to a new leader.

  What happens during the transition if the company does not have shared culture and values? In that case, you have three likely scenarios. 1.) The new leader has similar values to the previous leader, thus maintains the status quo. 2.) The new leader prefers the top to spin to the left, even though functionally it is the same as spinning to the right. Despite the leader's preference, upon evaluating the situation, decides to maintain status quo. 3.) The new leader, with a preference for the top to spin to the left, stops the top despite the current momentum and restarts it to the left.

  Now let's consider the company that has a shared culture and values. They have a well-defined system in which leaders operate so during a transition there is little deviation (*everyone knows the top is supposed to spin to the right*) therefore the momentum is not significantly affected.

- **Very few 'too good to be true' or 'get rich quick' business opportunities work out.**

  I often had a thought when I was working for the owners, who were constantly trying these schemes. If I put one of those claw vending machines at the end of the owner's driveway and charge $5 a shot to pick up a $100 bill lying flat on the bottom, I could be a millionaire as they could never pass up the machine without trying.

  This said, nobody would believe these schemes if someone didn't occasionally get rich. I have seen it for myself. In business, this happens when someone stumbles into lots of money with little to no effort. Keep in mind, though, most people who are extremely successful in business work extremely hard (*and having some good luck has never hurt anyone*).

Bridging the Gap

Leadership Style: Bureaucratic

The bureaucratic leadership style is characterized by a clear chain of command, rigid rules and regulations, and employee conformance.

A bureaucratic leader embraces a chain of command with clearly defined roles and responsibilities for each level of the organization. They seek to put the most appropriate person in each position.

Bureaucratic leaders embrace a merit based system. Employees are led based on their skillset, competency, performance, and adherence to the rules and regulations. Companies that chose to install bureaucratic leaders must operate with a structured set of rules, regulations, processes, and procedures.

The advantages of the bureaucratic leadership style are:

- **Predictable work environment**

- **Increased job security for employees**

- Removes leadership bias

- Employee opportunities based on merit

- Clear roles, responsibilities, and expectations

- Highly structured and functional operating system

Disadvantages of the bureaucratic leadership style are:

- Inefficient with all decisions and approvals going through leader

- Stagnates innovation and creativity

- Lack of collaboration or relationship building

- Company becomes rigid and unwilling to change

"Time is irreplaceable, therefore anything you spend time on that doesn't add value should be avoided, modified, or eliminated."

– Tim Marsh

Chapter 22:

Empty Suits

"You are best served by developing specific interview questions and tasks that allow you to see a candidate's core personality traits and competencies."

– Tim Marsh

Contemplations:

- *Recall a time in which you worked with someone who was not competent for their position. Why were they incompetent? Do you know how they obtained their position? What impact did their incompetence have?*

- *Have you ever knowingly over exaggerated your qualifications? Did you benefit from this? Were there any adverse effects? How did knowingly over exaggerating your qualifications make you feel?*

FORTUNATE FOR BRANDON, HE ISN'T PAID TO THINK.

The Story...

Location: ■■■■ *(Redacted)*

Over the past twenty plus years, I have had the privilege of working with some truly outstanding men and women. Their competency and performance have been outstanding. I also have had to work with more than a few empty suits.

These are people who outwardly appear to be something better than reality. In general, these empty suits fall into two types. The first type is those who know their image is a façade (*these people typically manipulate and exploit and then move on before they are called out, leaving a trail of damage throughout a multitude of companies*). The second type is disillusioned, they actually believe their competencies and performance actually match their outward appearance.

I had the opportunity to work with a couple of empty suits (*turned out to be father and son*) two separate times with the same company. It started even before I worked for the company, and then two more times after I was an employee.

The first time I met Dick was after I was approached to do some consulting by Wally, one of the company's sales employees (*I had worked with in the past*). We lined up a meeting at the office to discuss the project with Dick (*the company's general manager*).

My qualifications and experience had been communicated to Dick by Wally. It didn't take long after I arrived at the meeting for Dick to start his spiel. From the start, I could tell he felt threatened by me.

Dick discussed how he brought the company idea to the owner, David. How all of the customers were his. How he ran all of the jobs. How he organized and purchased all of the equipment. How he named the company. How he did all of the policies and procedures. How he developed all of the paperwork and manuals (*which were copied from other companies or from consultants*). How he and David were partners. (*Note that I don't refer to him as an owner. He wasn't even though that was what he wanted everyone to think. David is a fair and decent man who had promised him and several others a percentage of the company should it ever sell. He took that as meaning he was an owner.)* It went on and on. It was at that point I also found out that outside of Wally, everyone else at the company were his family members *(one of which also turned out to be an empty suit while the other was the real deal that facilitated him being able to go as far as he had).*

I came away from the meeting having been told all that he had done and how important he was to the company. The problem was that I really didn't know what he wanted from me. I don't think he knew of what he wanted from me.

Ultimately, I received marching orders from Wally. Shortly after completing the consulting work, I was looking to transition away from the company I was working for at the time. Due to having a non-compete, I needed to be outside of the industry for several years, and this company fit that bill for what I was looking for, so I asked Wally to arrange a meeting with me and David.

The meeting occurred at lunch, with Dick and Wally also in attendance. It was obvious to me that Dick was not on board with my potential hire, as his tone was overly aggressive during the lunch.

He is a large guy that used physical intimidation as one of his tactics. Since I'm bigger than Dick *(and not physically intimidated)*, this compounded him feeling threatened.

I have worked a long time at the skill of keeping a very professional manner when conducting business in adverse or adversarial conditions. Thus, I am rarely unable to control my language and temper in a business setting. As the lunch progressed, the tension between Dick and me grew. Not only was it now apparent that he was threatened by me but also that he did not like me (*that feeling was mutual as he was two things that I really don't like, an empty suit and a bully*). At one point, the conversation between him and I got very tense and heated. While I was not happy that I had gotten upset, I did feel that given the situation I was able to control myself and I ended by telling him something to the effect that I wouldn't presume to know his business (*i.e., specialization*) if he likewise wouldn't presume to know mine.

Despite the tension with Dick, I did end up accepting a job with the company, reporting directly to David. Unknown to all of us at the time, Dick had been working behind the scenes to take all of the company's customers (*it was a very small company with only a few customers*) and his family members to start-up another company with another financial backer (*this time even though he did not contribute any money, he was given a minority ownership of the new company*).

Closing the Gap

LEADERSHIP TIP 22:

Keep meetings productive by focusing on topics that impact your customers.

About a week after I started, he executed his plan (*it is worth mentioning that at this point, I didn't have enough exposure to his son to realize that he too was an empty suit*). The result was that Wally and I were the only two employees left. Neither of us had experience with the products and services the company sold. With no field employees and no customers, we were left to rebuild the company. This was the first time I worked with them.

The company was located in east Texas and about seven hours away from where the owner had his primary business in south Texas. I was now running the company. While the story is likely interesting enough for its own book, the gist is that we made many mistakes while trying to rebuild. Some of these were due to the company we inherited, and many due to our own miscalculations.

Ultimately, we made the decision to move the company's operations to south Texas in order to take advantage of the synergies with the owners other business. This was a very easy business decision and a difficult one personally. My family and I lived in east Texas for seven years (*the longest I had lived anywhere since leaving my parents' house*) and we were hesitant to move to south Texas. As a result, I commuted weekly for a year and a half before capitulating and moving my family to south Texas. In retrospect, this year and a half period was not only extremely hard on me and my family but also to the detriment of the company.

Eventually, despite many false starts, the company started rebuilding and was on the path to becoming profitable. We had started reaping the synergies we anticipated between the two companies even with a prolonged industry downturn hampering our efforts.

Despite Dick's efforts to destroy the company, he and David kept in touch. As expected, the promises of success and profits that he had sold to his new partner weren't true. Eventually, their relationship soured and Dick learned that being a minority owner brought little ability to control the company's direction. The majority owner cut the pay of all employees (*including Dick*) and in time that company folded. This brings us to the second time that I worked with these two empty suits.

After the collapse of his business, Dick began talking to David (*I was involved in the conversations*). In these conversations, he was much humbler and gave the impression that he may have calmed some of his previously aggressive ways (*although I never believed that he had changed*). He claimed to have work that should they (*he and his family members*) return; we could cover. Both David and I were hesitant, however we also knew that the additional work could help us through the downturn. After a while, despite misgivings on both our parts, we decided to move forward with a small satellite location in east Texas with them as the only employees (*with him being sales/management*).

At first, things were better, however there were huge logistical challenges supporting the location. Initially, his son, Dick, Jr. (*who was hired as the location manager*) would meet me halfway to minimize the driving. Eventually, he started making excuses as to why he couldn't meet halfway, and I had to make the entire trip (*by this time I was fully aware the apple didn't fall far from the tree, especially in this case*).

PERSONAL BACKSTORY: Even though I was the company's Vice President, I have never minded doing whatever it takes to make things happen. Since I have always run my operations very lean (*by choice*), I was the one who could and was willing to drive all night to deliver tools and equipment. Having just moved to south Texas to avoid the seven-hour drive, I found myself making the trip more than before I moved.

It didn't take long for things to turn south. Even though the revenue was sufficient to be profitable, their salaries were low (*as he voluntarily set them low initially in order to entice David to bring them aboard*). It wasn't long before he was wanting a new facility (*we had rented half of the facility we had vacated when we had moved to south Texas*), more tools and equipment, and a raise in his salary. For a period of time, David resisted, but eventually he capitulated and raised the salaries (*although the raises were still lower than what the employees had been making before they left the first time*). Over time, we also allocated more and more equipment to the operation.

The equipment was a source of frustration. In his role as location manager, there was little for Dick, Jr. to do other than to make sure the equipment was ready for a job and maintained. Each time I arrived at the facility, the equipment was in poor condition. Dick, Jr. claimed he was too busy to clean things up, but I knew their volume and didn't buy into his claims. In addition, the landlord (*who occupied the other half of the building*) often told me that he didn't spend much time at the facility.

The whole situation leveraged me to be in the middle. I was desperately wanting the revenue in order to grow the company yet was being taken advantage of by both of these guys (*the third family member was the one actually doing the work*). I was willing to be played in the short-term while the revenue was generating profits, however eventually the work started slowing.

As the profits dropped, things started to get much worse. Father and son was now being placed under pressure, and neither had the ability or motivation to do that which was necessary to pull out of the downward spiral.

David and I differed on the correct course of action. Having been leveraged for so long, I was ready to cut our loses and move forward. David wanted to see if we could salvage the operation. In the end, we reduced costs through salary reductions to attempt to salvage the operation. Ultimately, this didn't work. Dick ended up quitting, and I ended up terminating Dick, Jr. We tried to keep the third family member as he was the one actually generating the revenue, but ultimately he resigned to accept another position. At this point, the satellite location closed.

From a business perspective, the entire endeavor netted very little profit for the company, however did help with cashflow through a difficult downturn period. We were also able to increase our asset inventory through the process (*which in lieu of profits were the upside*).

The whole endeavor really took a toll on me personally. It included the stress of leading such a low quality team (*not including the field supervisor*) driving all night on more occasions than I could count to deliver equipment, and listening to Dick, Jr. lie during his unemployment hearing that he worked sixty plus hours a week.

...and the Lessons Learned:

- **WHEN POSSIBLE, PAUSE AND REFLECT IN TIMES OF BUSINESS ADVERSITY.**
  When faced with a crisis of the magnitude that could jeopardize the survival of your company, you must resist the temptation to act immediately. Instead, the prudent course of action is to pause and reflect.

  This will give you the opportunity to fully evaluate your situation and then develop a well-thought-out course of action. By following this process, you can avoid the pitfalls many of us who haven't suffered as a result of our knee jerk, scatter shot responses.

- ### People rarely change their core personality traits.

In this example, Dick was argumentative, arrogant, and aggressive the first time he worked for the company. However, when he was talking with David about coming back the second time, he was meek and humble, a changed man. He was in fact not a changed man, and simply was putting on a false persona when talking with the owner in order to accomplish his objective. During difficult times, this false persona gave way to his core personality, which had not changed. Eventually, after many occurrences of this, he gave up and returned to his true personality.

This is an important lesson as false personas often appear during the new hire interview process. These may be for the benefit or detriment of the candidate.

An example of a candidate benefiting would be one who, although usually pessimistic and negative, intentionally appears to be happy and positive. This candidate, if hired, may do a good job, but their personality may bring down the entire team.

An example where the candidate is hindered would be a well-qualified, introverted candidate that becomes so nervous in an interview that they are unable to respond effectively. In this case the best candidate may be overlooked.

You are best served by developing specific interview questions and tasks that allow you to see a candidate's core personality traits and competencies.

Bridging the Gap
Discipline

The term 'discipline' often has a negative connotation. In business, this is reinforced when it is used primarily as a tool to punish or terminate employees.

In order to maximize the potential of your employees, first and foremost, you must see and believe that progressive discipline is an opportunity to correct and modify your employees' performance to align it with your mission, values, and objectives.

A common pitfall with discipline is the inequities that occur. For example, leaders are frequently hesitant to discipline high performing employees, whereas poor performing employees are disciplined without pause. Why is this? The obvious answer is that leaders do not want to risk disenfranchising or losing their high performers (*thus may allow issues to linger or slide*).

In contrast, with low performing employees, leaders may quite frankly not care whether they stay or actually hope they quit (*thus have no hesitation to issue discipline*).

This subjective discipline based on employee performance high-lights serious leadership deficiencies while simultaneously under-mining the effectiveness of the progressive discipline system. It should not be the mechanism used to compensate for inadequate or deficient hiring practices and personnel management.

Chapter 23:

Creating a Mirage

"Without a doubt, creating a mirage not based on truth or reality falls on the wrong side of the line with respect to ethics and integrity."

– Tim Marsh

Contemplations:

- *Recall a time in which you told a false-hood (this is a nice way of saying you lied) in order to get out of trouble. Did it work? Were there any consequences? How did telling the falsehood make you feel?*

- *Have you ever been intentionally misled by someone for their own agenda? Did they achieve the deception? Were there any consequences for their actions? How did being intentionally misled make you feel?*

WOODY IS CONTEMPLATING IF IT'S STILL OR SPARKLING.

The Story...
Location: Various

What is a mirage? You've likely seen the western where the cowboy is stranded in the desert. As he walks, he sees a lifesaving pool of water only to find out it was an illusion, a mirage. In this case, the mirage was caused naturally by heat (*and a lot of hope*).

In business, the intent of a mirage is influence perception by intentionally misleading or positioning circumstances in a manner to attempt to affect an outcome. These efforts incorporate a mixture of impressions, egos, biases, and desires to accomplish a desired result. As you can see in the following examples, people create mirages for various reasons, often justified (*at least in their minds*), but nonetheless not necessarily the whole story or accurate.

PERSONAL BACKSTORY: While managing the northeast, I used to tell the employees with company vehicles to leave their doors unlocked. This way, maybe a thief would feel sorry for them and throw a cassette or CD player (*this was before the MP3 player days*) in the vehicle. Our vehicles were basic to say the least. They were plain white with no power locks, no power windows, no carpet, no chrome, and an AM-FM radio.

Example 1 – I remember asking Ben who used to manage the business before selling out (*he was also one of the owners*) why the company vehicles were so plain. Even the management and owner's vehicles were as simple and cheap as possible.

He explained to me that they specifically ordered the vehicles that way (*at a higher cost than the basic models available on the lot*). The purpose was because they didn't want their customers to think they were making too much profit. This allowed them to keep their pricing higher. The fact was that before selling out, their business operated with over 50% field profit.

Example 2 – Within six weeks of assuming the additional responsibility for the Department of Transportation (DOT) compliance, we received a letter informing us of a upcoming audit. At the time, I was juggling the responsibilities of what six weeks earlier had been the full time jobs for two people.

I had met my DOT compliance staff and remember being briefed on the outstanding issues. I had not yet delved into resolving them at the point in which we received the letter.

My first efforts after being informed with the audit was to get fully briefed on the audit process and to assess our position. The compliance staff painted a grim picture. I decided to bring in an outside consultant (*someone who was a former auditor*) to perform a mock audit.

When I walked into the debriefing meeting, I asked the contract auditor what the verdict was. "You're (censored)!" he said. You will receive an unsatisfactory rating.

When I asked him what that meant, he went on to tell me that we would have literally a few weeks to resolve the issues and if not we would lose our operating authority. Losing this would be catastrophic to the business, to say the least.

When I sat down with my manager to give him the update, he obviously was as concerned as I was. To his credit, rather than lament the poor performance of my predecessor that contributed to the challenges, he accepted them and gave me full support to get the issues resolved.

We caught a break when the auditor called and asked if it was alright if he delayed the audit a month. I told him it would be fine. This was what we needed. Needless to say, the next month was rough. We were getting in stacks of training documents, maintenance documents, and other paperwork every day. In some way, it was awesome to see how things came together to get so much accomplished. This just goes to show the benefits of effective leadership.

Beyond the efforts to fix the issues, we went to work finding out all we could about the auditor. When he finally arrived to conduct the audit, Zach (*my DOT compliance manager*) welcomed him in his office. Since in our research we had found out both the auditor and Zach were former state troopers, I had asked Zack to bring in a few extra mementos to festoon his office. As expected, they spent the first hour or so talking about their previous assignments, shared connections, etc.

Closing ▷◁ **the Gap**

LEADERSHIP TIP 23:

Seek to honor and preserve traditions while building a better future.

Our DOT compliance assistant was a motherly type who brought freshly baked goods to work. These baked goods and an assortment of drinks and snacks were set up in the conference room for the auditor.

In addition to the food and drink spread, we had much of the documentation that we knew he would be asking for already arranged on the conference room table. This way, when he asked for it, we had the documents easily available.

Our operation consisted of thirty plus locations. When it came to needing a random sample of vehicle files, we happened to have some in the office that we had been working on that we offered the auditor. This convenience prevented the need for us to overnight files from the locations. As it happened, all of the files we had on hand were in pristine compliance. We also had pre-screened a large quantity of logbooks. When the auditor asked for a number of sample logbooks, we gave him the pre-screen ones.

None of our efforts to create a mirage were outside of the law. We simply used familiarity, perception of readiness and competency, and his desire for convenience to our advantage. We created the mirage and the auditor walked towards it. The result was we passed the audit with a satisfactory rating (*the highest available*).

The question now is ethics and integrity. The longer I am in business, the more I appreciate these qualities and realize they are not as common as I expected.

I can make arguments on both sides of the ethics case for this example. I truly wish that I was never put in the position where there was uncertainty of the outcome, had we not positioned ourselves the way we did.

The overreaching question is had we not done the things we did to position ourselves during the audit, would we have still received a satisfactory rating? Perhaps. That's something that can never be known.

What I prefer to consider with respect to the audit ethics and integrity is that we changed as an organization (*in hindsight we were on the wrong side of the line but made the business life or death decision necessary*).

If anything does ease my conscience, it is that we worked diligently from the time of the letter going forward to do things right, and this continued after the audit concluded. Our compliance commitment was real and lasting.

...and the Lessons Learned:

- **MANAGEMENT SUPPORT OF INITIATIVES IS CRITICAL FOR SUCCESS.**
  Any company initiative is easier to accomplish with management support. Primarily, this support comes in two forms.

  The first is the visible commitment of management for the initiative. Typically, the bigger the initiative, the higher level of management that is required to provide support. In most cases, the simple task of communicating their support can have a tremendous effect within the company. The public support influences actions, behaviors, and priorities of employees. In cases where external support is necessary, management leading the initiative's cheerleading efforts actively demonstrates the company's commitment level.

The second type is when management puts into action their visible commitment. This includes dedicating time to the initiative, making decisions that support the employees responsible for execution, and allocating any required money, assets, or people.

- **CREATING A MIRAGE CHALLENGES ETHICS AND INTEGRITY.**
In most cases, creating a mirage (*or perception*) not based on truth falls on the wrong side of the line with respect to ethics and integrity. This includes creating a mirage with the intent to not convey the entire story.

I fully understand and sympathize with the existential dilemma when placed in a business life or death situation. To avoid this, leaders should assess their business for these risks and proactively address them before being put in the situation.

Bridging the Gap
Attitude vs. Aptitude

It is important to understand the cause of an employee not satisfactorily performing their assigned tasks and responsibilities. In the simplest form, the causes can be classified as attitude, aptitude, or in some cases a combination.

An attitude cause is when an employee has the skillset and ability to do the assigned tasks and responsibilities, but for whatever reason they choose not to because of an emotional or motivation difficulty.

Attitude causes may or may not be work related and can vary from relationship problems to money. An aptitude cause is when an employee is not able to complete their assigned tasks and responsibilities due to a lack of knowledge, physical ability, or job tools and resources.

Causes of aptitude issues tend to be work related, however in some specific cases, they may be non-work related. Work related issues vary from lack of training to not having the tools to complete the job. An example of a non-work related aptitude issue is an injury that occurs outside of work.

An example combination issue would be an employee that has an overall negative attitude due to consistently not having access to the proper tools and resources needed to complete their job tasks and responsibilities.

> "With the technology available to the modern workforce, it's advantageous to focus on the efficiency, performance, and results of your employees versus punctuality and attendance."
>
> – TIM MARSH

Chapter 24:

Leadership Test

"Due diligence and homework are often the keys to success in business."

– TIM MARSH

Contemplations:

- *Consider a time when you received a tip or some information that gave you an advantage. Did you know the value of the information at the time? Did you solicit the information or was it given to you?*

- *Have you ever experienced short-term failure, only to have the experience lead to a long-term benefit? Was the benefit due to how the failure was handled?*

Mind the Gap

THE CAPTAIN IS THINKING IT MIGHT BE TOO
LATE TO GET BUY-IN ON HIS LAST DECISION.

The Story...

Location: Missouri

PERSONAL BACKSTORY: In the late 90s, St. Louis, Missouri had one, if not the only, floating McDonald's restaurant. While the restaurant has since closed, I can still clearly remember being outside looking at the Mississippi River as I was having the phone conversation that changed my life.

I was talking to one of the recruiting assistants for my upcoming second interview in Houston. I remember asking her what I can expect. I don't know why she did it, but she ended up giving me most of the interview details. The interview would be a group interview involving a number of candidates. The recruiters' objective, she said, was to determine whether any of the candidates had leadership capabilities.

It was a real epiphany for me. Prior to that conversation, I assumed it would be another one-on-one interview focused on getting to know me better, possibly exploring my education and skills in more detail. Considering how introverted I was at the time, had I not been given this information in advance, there is no way I would have been successful with the interview. It's not that I didn't have leadership abilities, in fact I was in a supervisory position at the time, it was just that I typically would not have been outgoing enough within a group of strangers to adequately demonstrate these skills.

Armed with the knowledge they were looking for leadership abilities, I entered the interview with a much different strategy as I would normally. I was outgoing (*at that time, I usually needed to get comfortable with people before this would occur*).

There were two exercises I remember completing, along with the other candidates. In retrospect, the information the assistant gave me was spot on, as they were both clearly designed to prompt leaders to step forward and guide the groups.

The first exercise was outside and involved all the candidates (*there were twenty or so*) being blindfolded. A rope was then placed in each of our hands. The recruiters told us that we had to make a square with the rope, working with the other candidates attached to the rope. We could move our hands along the rope, but could not release the rope with either hand. They did not tell us how many groups there were. The time limit was twenty minutes or so, and the recruiters said they were going inside for a break.

Obviously, the recruiters were standing back to watch who stepped up to lead the efforts.

Guess who was one of the candidates that stepped up to take the lead of the situation?

Correct, it was moi!

I was at the forefront of the leadership efforts. First, I had to deter-mine how many people were attached to my rope. To do this, I had to ask each of the other candidates to slide their hands left and right until they either bumped into someone else's hand or reach an end. One candidate had an end and then everyone else seemed to bump into another person. Well, that didn't make any sense, the rope obviously had to have two ends. We worked on that dilemma until we determined that three people were bumping a hand up against what felt like a knot. *A lasso*, I thought, *the rope was shaped like a lasso with a loop and a straight section coming off.* Tricky, very tricky I thought.

We eventually had the candidates on the free-end of the lasso to bring their rope up and double up their rope with that of the main loop. Meanwhile, the other candidates slid down to make room. This essentially made the lasso into a circle. We then worked to determine how many of us were attached to the rope. I started with one and had the person to the right of me count two and we continued that process until the person to the left of me bumped me. Turns out, we were all attached to the same rope.

Now, we moved on to the task of making a square. The plan was that me and three others would make 90 degree angles with our hands and back up until the rope was stretched (*since we counted out, we knew how many people were on the rope thus divided the rope up based on people to get approximately the same length sides*). We worked at this a while until time was called. While not a square, it was not a circle either when they asked us to all lay down the rope and take off our blindfolds.

I felt pretty good that I was showing leadership after the first exercise. We had some other tasks that day, including IQ type comprehension tests. The day concluded with an open bar dinner at the hotel. Each recruiter sat at a table with place cards for the candidates. While dubbed as a casual dinner, I was quite aware that our actions were being closely observed.

The next day brought about the second exercise. The objective was to build a device that would be dropped from the second floor balcony and protect an egg from being broken. The caveat was that the egg had to be physically touching the ground once it landed. We were split into groups of 4 or 5 and given supplies along with scissors. These supplies included paper, scotch tape, string, and a balloon. A time limit was set and we started.

Again, knowing they were watching us for leadership qualities, I pushed forward with a design that I thought would work well. It consisted of a tube of paper attached to the inflated balloon, with a parachute attached to the tube. The concept was simple. First, the egg would be inserted into the tube before being dropped. While in free-fall, the parachute would slow down the whole device, while the inflated balloon would cushion the egg on impact. Once it landed, it would fall over and the egg would simply roll down the tube onto the floor. In theory, the design seemed solid, and the entire team agreed to proceed with this our course of action.

Execution of the design went well, and I was so proud of the device as it looked excellent as we all walked up the stairs (*unfortunately this was in a time before phones with cameras and social media, so no pictures*). We were third in the order of groups to drop.

The first group dropped their device and smash, the egg was pulverized. I have to admit, I probably had a smug look on my face, as I was thinking we were going to nail it.

The second team's device looked like a third-grader built it. Again, I likely was smug as ours was beautiful. They dropped their egg and, success! I really couldn't believe that they had achieved the objective. Nonetheless, I was still confident. Now it was our time.

Closing the Gap

LEADERSHIP TIP 24:

Focus on building your team, not only for today, but also for the future.

I can remember one of our team members held the tube and dropped the egg down in it while the other held the parachute. Then, on the count of three, they dropped it. The next few seconds seemed to last an eternity. The first indication of a problem was when the parachute did not work at all to slow the device. It literally dropped like a rock. The balloon worked exactly as predicted, absorbing the impact of the egg. What we had not anticipated was the amount of energy absorbed. When the energy rebounded, it shot the egg about twelve feet straight up out of the tube into the air. The egg seemed to hang in suspension forever before falling to a spectacular splattering.

The laughter was quick and prolonged. I still remember all the blood flowing to my face. I suspect I was as red as a beet from embarrassment. All I could think was, *there goes my chances for a job.*

I can't remember how the other groups did, as I was in a daze (*perhaps shock*). Later, one of the recruiters came up to me and told me that in all of the times they had done that exercise, they had never seen an egg do what ours did. I was aghast.

I recovered and finished the day up as best I could. We were told as we departed that we would receive a letter in the mail with the results of the interview and whether or not we would be invited to a field location for a third interview. I can remember thinking that my chances of that were slim to none.

As it turns out, I was wrong. I did get the opportunity for a third interview. Eventually, I was offered a position with the company.

...and the Lessons Learned:

- **THE 'RIGHT' INFORMATION IS A COMPETITIVE ADVANTAGE.**
  With all the information available in the world today (*and keep in mind that the amount of information created is growing exponentially*), it is essential to be able to ascertain what is the '*right*' information. The basic definition of this would be any information that you can use to assist with achieving a positive result.

  In the case of my interview, doing my homework, being diligent, and following up with the assistant paid off with several key pieces of information.

  Keep in mind that the easiest way to get the '*right*' information is to ask the right questions. While asking the right questions may not always produce results, one thing is for sure: not asking questions will limit the amount of information. Sometimes the 'right' information is given to you (*either on purpose or by accident*). Even with these somewhat random events, your conversations may be affected by factors such as your previous actions, reputation, or simply being in the right place at the right time.

Due diligence and homework are often the keys to success in business. Take for example a sales meeting with a client you have never met. Online searches, calling a mutual acquaintance, or other research can provide you with information that can make the difference between success and failure. Social media can give you valuable information about family, alma mater, personal interests, etc. Often some of this information is available once you enter their office by simply looking at the pictures hanging on the wall or items on their desk.

Irrespective of how you gather the *'right'* information (*assuming you maintain your integrity*), consider how using it effectively can lead to your success.

■ **MAKE CALCULATED DECISIONS.**
Often people will say *'take a calculated risk'*. Practically, I find risk to be a tough discussion point because everyone has a different tolerance level. To explain this better, consider that unless comprehensive criteria are established, what I may consider high risk you may consider low risk. Thus, we are not talking apples to apples.

Perhaps this is why I prefer to say calculated decision. These mitigate the unknowns by incorporating information and logic into the decision (*this may be circular logic if you consider these unknowns as risks*). A third component incorporated into decisions is your intuition (*i.e. your gut feelings*).

I find that intuition comes from self-reflection of your experiences. While not always reliable, intuition is important and most people use it more than they realize. Intuition is often how we handle the unknown portion of decisions. How many times in school did you answer a question you really didn't know that answer to, then change your answer upon second guessing yourself, only to have the original answer be correct? Your intuition was the first answer.

So how does this relate to my second interview? I knew that the recruiters were looking for leadership traits, but I didn't know the exercises that we would face. I had never been in either of these situations, so I had to take the information I was given and then use logic and my intuition to make decisions.

The results of the calculated decisions made in the first exercise were successful. In the second exercise, the results weren't successful, however the recruiters appreciated that the design was produced using methodical calculated decisions. While I am not saying that as long as the process is correct the results don't matter, I am saying that with a methodical process, the chances of obtaining successful results are higher.

"If employment candidates already understand and share the company's core values, the likelihood for retention increases."

– Tim Marsh

Mind the Gap:

Recommended Author List

Over the years, I've read extensively in an effort to develop my leadership, sales, and business skills from others. In my experience, books and other publications (both electronic and written) are an inexpensive and readily available resource for developing leadership skills.

It's not possible to list every author of an excellent business and leadership book. The criteria I used was authors whose book contributed significantly to my skill development.

These authors are:

- **Ken Blanchard/Spencer Johnson**
- **Larry Bossidy/Ram Charan**
- **Dale Carnegie**
- **Jim Collins**
- **Stephen Covey**
- **Peter Drucker**
- **Jeffrey Gitomer**
- **Adam Grant**
- **Napoleon Hill**
- **Walter Isaacson**
- **John Maxwell**
- **Jack Welch**
- **Zig Ziglar**

About the Author

My life has taken many twists and turns over the years, for which I could have never planned or predicted. This book is yet another one…

I grew up in a blue-collar family in Illinois. At sixteen, I started my first job. I worked there throughout high school and college. After graduating from Southern Illinois University with a mechanical engineering degree, I started in the Texas oilfield.

I have worked various operational and support positions at both large and small companies. Besides living in Texas (*in five different locations throughout the state*), Oklahoma, and West Virginia (*twice in Charleston*), my family and I have also lived and worked in Canada. Additionally, I have traveled to Venezuela, Mexico, Abu Dhabi, England and extensively throughout the United States for business.

Throughout my career, from field to executive level positions, I find that I have been an unwitting student of leadership and management techniques.

Melanie (*my beautiful wife and a wonderful mother to our children*) and I met at work while we were both going to school. We were married shortly after I graduated from SIU. We currently reside in Corpus Christi, Texas with our six children (*Katelyn, Jay, Ben, Emily, Carter, and Ethan*) and three dogs (*Cocoa, Annie, and Ella*).

In my spare time, I enjoy church activities, spending time with my family, being outdoors, working on new product designs, and my newest passion, being an author.

This book is dedicated to my parents, Sharon and Alfred (1936-2012), Melanie, my kids, and all of my friends that have supported me…

Now, having read this book...

Do you see how powerful learning from others' accomplishments, miscalculations, and failures can be in your leadership development?

To be successful in business, your answer has to be YES...!

Remember that it is up to you to define success and the priorities in your life. Never stop learning, always do your best, and enjoy life.